# *Reliving* Sujatha

## His best stories in English

# *Reliving*

# Sujatha

## His best stories in English

Translator
Vimala Balakrishnan

Vitasta

*Let Knowledge Spread*

Published by
Renu Kaul Verma
Vitasta Publishing Pvt Ltd
2/15, Ansari Road, Daryaganj
New Delhi - 110 002
info@vitastapublishing.com

ISBN 978-93-82711-95-7



First Edition 2017
Third Reprint 2022

MRP 350



Typeset by Vits Press
Printed by Vikas Computer and Printers

Sujatha is one of those few writers who continuously wrote widely read novels. If the undercurrent of subtle humour made him most popular among young readers, his ability to give detailed and lively description about anything on earth made him a favourite of serious readers.

Sujatha was the most successful writer in Tamil cinema. He had collaborated with the best of film-makers and directors, like Balachandar, Mani Ratnam, Bharatiraja, Kamal Haasan and Shankar, and ensured that their films are enjoyed for dialogues also.

**www.indiaglitz.com/kamal-hasan-mani-ratnam-shankar-writer-sujatha-81st-birth-anniversary-tamil-news-138191.html**

# Contents

# Publisher's Note

In our quest to bring vernacular literature to the mainstream through our Relive Series (*Reliving Indira Goswami* and *Reliving Tagore*), we came across S Rangarajan who penned under his wife's name Sujatha. He has been one of the most popular writers of Tamil fiction, featured in several magazines.

Later he contributed as script/screenplay writer for several Tamil movies. He also immortalized Ganesh-Vasanth—an imaginary advocate pair serving as the main characters in most of his detective stories. In the movie *Priya*, his fictional character Ganesh, was played by Rajnikanth. Kamal Haasan's *Vikram* was composed by him. He penned dialogues for the movie *Roja* directed by Mani Ratnam.

Since we believe that regional authors should also be read across the country, we accepted the translated stories brought by Vimla Balakrishnan and decided to publish them. The stories are edited by Veena Batra.

This book tells us stories that catch the reader unawares with unexpected twists and turns filling them with awe, shock, and horror. Through this book, we hope that readers will relive the legacy of his special art of story-telling.

**Renu Kaul Verma**

# Translator's Note

After reading a number of stories of Sujatha, I felt many of them deserved a wider audience. The growing number of expatriate Tamilians, who speak the language but can't read popular writings in Tamil, may like to read Sujatha, and through him, gain insights into a world that is familiar and yet distant.

Initially, I thought of writing a biography of Sujatha, introducing him to English-speaking readers. As I read more, and spoke to others familiar with his works, my initial idea evolved to introducing the author through translation of his short stories and novellas.

While I was familiar with some of Sujatha's short stories, selecting from his vast body of work for this collection, and then translating the stories, required a different kind of research support.

The Tamil Sangam's library in New Delhi, and especially the librarian, Ms R Shameen Unnissa, was a source of support. She helped locate novels by Sujatha, and also got in touch with publishers to source books that were hard to locate. Some of the stories in this collection are part of his work on science and medicine. My brother Dr Venkatesh, and Dr Priti Dutt, helped clarify medical terms and expressions, and eased the process of translating scientific terminology, accurately.

Mrs Sujatha Rangarajan, in consultation with her sons, Rangaprasad and Kesava Prasad, supported the idea, giving me a free hand to select from his works, providing the rights to translate and publish.

Renu Kaul Verma of Vitasta Publishing and editor Veena Batra invested time and creative energy to bring this book to you.

But none of this would have been possible without my family, my husband, children, daughter-in-law, and above all my grandchildren, without whose encouragement this book would not have seen the light of day.

I hope the journey of reading this collection of short stories will be as enjoyable as the process of getting them to you has been for me.

**Vimala Balakrishnan**

# Guru Prasad's Last Day

GURU PRASAD is one of the 10,000 workers in the factory. 27 years old. Married a year back and his wife is in a delicate condition, an expectant mother. His friends call him Guru. He has very few friends. They are his colleagues, KP Srinivasa Murthy, Anjaneyappa, Dominique and the house owner's son, Satyanarayana.

Guru Prasad is almost like a machine. He is a senior rivet strikng mechanic, who goes to the factory every day in the factory bus and who, with neither a liking nor a care or interest, strikes the machine which goes rivet, rivet, rivet, rivet…non-stop, the whole day. He is an exalted, eight years experienced rivet. What is the eight years experience? Just stand next to a machine to supervise its function and press a button. If a green light shines, press another button and wait till a bell rings or a red light glows and then stop it.

This way a man becomes an integral part of a machine. In the factory there are so many such functions for a man which are an essential part of the machine. There is plenty of such work in a factory. Any person with seven years experience in this work will automatically turn into a machine. You need not be surprised if you locate a socket to wind a key on his back. Guru Prasad is a senior mechanic. A worker. When he comes out of the factory, he is a man, a husband. There is nothing special about him. He is neither very handsome nor a great singer, or a great sportsman. There is nothing heroic about him. The whole story revolves around Guru Prasad's death.

Guru Prasad joined the factory when he was nineteen. His blood pressure had been high even at that time. When his medical was done, his high BP was not detected. Due to it, he used to get headaches and even dizziness for a few seconds, off and on. In the initial stages, it did not cause any problem for him. Whenever he had a headache, he used to go to factory dispensary and take either an asprin or a disprin. If he felt dizzy, he used to catch hold of whatever was handy at that time. Had some specialist checked his BP, he might have been furious. Having noticed the warning signals in his diastolic, he would have strongly recommended complete bed rest at once.

Guru Prasad's only visit to a doctor was to Rayar. He had been treating small children for the past twenty years. Hence, he had become an expert paediatrician, and his whole world comprised of wriggling worms in the stomach. His pet theory was that the world would be free of all diseases just by taking a dose of deworming medicine. When Guru Prasad went to him, he gave him a dark, tea coloured mixture and said that when his stomach cleared, he would become normal. Guru had severe diarrhea, but didn't suffer from dizziness for a few days. When he had dizziness the next time, he, on his own, took a laxative as well as Antipar worm medicine. In the meanwhile, his BP kept going up steadily.

Last year, Guru Prasad's marriage was solemnized. The marriage was held in Kottai Srinivasa Perumal temple. Saraswathy was almost as tall as him. Guru Prasad's landlord spoke to Tumkoor Narayana Rao about him. He was recommended very strongly by the landlord. The boy has a permanent job in a factory, earns six hundred rupees per month and is a very good boy. Naryana Rao met Guru Prasad's parents for an alliance for his daughter, Saraswathy. They all liked her. The horoscopes matched well. The astrologer said both *suamangli praptam* and *mangalya praptam* (related to the longevity of husband) and the tallying of horoscopes was excellent. In short, no marriage could have been finalized this quickly. In exactly five weeks, Guru Prasad married Saraswathy and settled with her in the upstairs flat. There was no leave to go on a honeymoon. They invaded all the theatres in the city and kept awake all night. Saraswathy had her menses just once after the wedding. Guru possessed Saraswathy with a fierce passion and an urgency. When he lay on her fully, she used to feel suffocated. She used to wait for it to be over and as soon as he got off her fully satisfied, she used to sleep with great relief.

At the beginning of our story, Saraswathy is well advanced in her pregnancy with a rounded stomach and rounded face. She was beautiful to look at. She embroidered all available pillow slips with 'Welcome'. She was in the final stages of her pregnancy and was in the state of uncertainty that the delivery of the child could be at any time. Now…

The First Day

Guru and Saraswathy had been to Dr Sarada Pai that morning. Sarada Pai examined her and said that the position of the baby was okay and not to worry about the slight leaking liquid. She prescribed some tablets and said the delivery would take place within a week. Guru was about to consult her about his headache but her youthful appearance did not inspire confidence. A lady doctor should not be pretty. She should not powder her face or use lipstick. When she bent, her cleavage was visible. Guru was aroused because he had not had Saraswathy for a long time. He looked at his wife. She had dishevelled hair and her sari was tied up high. She had a crinkled forehead and, oh my god, what a big stomach! Is it a girl child? Let it be any child. It has to come out without giving much trouble. He asked the auto to be driven very slowly and brought Saraswathy back safely home. He went to the third block and sent a telegram to Saraswathy's mother to come immediately. He decided to have his headache checked properly when he passed ESI hospital the next time. A new doctor had been appointed and he was good in diagnosis. He must consult the factory doctor at least. The headache seemed to be one with him. It stuck to him. Something or the other had to be done. It was not advisable to postpone it for a long time. Why not take a day off and meet the doctor at ESI hospital? No, not today. Let the delivery be over. During delivery, lots of leave may have to be taken. It was not advisable to exhaust all the leave now itself.

As soon as he reached home, he lighted the kerosene stove and made coffee for both of them. Saraswathy pulled his hand to her stomach. He inserted his hand inside the sari and touched the warm stomach. He could feel the child kicking inside.

He said, "Hey Prasanna!"

"Are you sure the child is a boy?" she said with a smile and slept. He looked at the time. There was still an hour for the factory bus to arrive. Oh God! This headache! He decided to doze off for a short while. He had a dream. Unable to look after the twins, they leave one child with somebody. When they ask for the child to be returned, the request is flatly turned down. When he called out, "Prasanna, Prasanna", they could hear, "Dad, Dad," from inside the house.

He woke up with a start.. He splashed water on his face. He looked at Saraswathy. She was sleeping peacefully. He decided not to wake her up. He would lock the door from outside. It could be opened from inside too.

When Guru came out of the house he felt dizzy even before he could take ten steps but somehow he managed. He didn't pass a stool that morning. Hence, the headache.

By half-past-two, the factory's green bus came. He got into

the bus and as usual since the last four years, he went and sat on the seventh seat at the back. All the other workers either looked outside the window or read the paper and travelled in silence. One of the union members was speaking loudly. Some were enjoying his speeches because he was speaking about the manager in a very familiar manner.

Guru Prasad was looking outside. His gaze fell on a house just then and he resolved to buy one just like that. A smile played on his lips when he remembered the life he felt in Saraswathy's warm belly. Poor Saraswathy. Even in such an advanced stage of pregnancy, she cooks by sitting on a stool which is too small for her. Why can't her mother come a bit early? The daughter-in-law's delivery is already over. There were three recent births in their family. Saraswathy's elder brother's wife's sister Mano's second delivery. Besides, they were upset because he would not send Saraswathy to their place for the delivery. Does that city have better facilities than Bangalore? Saraswati's mother had to come to Bangalore positively. The child was definitely a son. He had to be named Guru Prasanna. All the names should have Guru. His father was Guru Raj. This boy is Guru Prasad's son, 'Guru Prasanna'........ "Guru!" "Guru!" "Guru!" Again and again, he repeated. He remembered Radha Jayalakshmi's record, "*Punarabi Jananam, Punarabi maranam*...."He remembered only that much. If the next life was asked, he could not answer because he didn't know. His reading was restricted to weekly magazines alone. He read a few *Vijaya Chitra* occasionally. In these also, mostly he glanced at the pictures. About ten seats away from him, he saw a girl with a *Filmfare* in her hand. The red cover alone could be seen. He had a sudden urge to see the magazine. He decided to buy a copy.

The factory bus terminus was almost similar to that of a city bus station. Guru got down slowly and mingled with the crowd. He showed his pass at the entrance, entered the huge concrete building, went to his shop which was inside, went to his section, and stood in front of his machine. He adjusted the height of the steel stool. The work which was left incomplete remained without a change. It waited for him to continue. He felt his bladder full. He came out of the shop. 'Working class unity, Zindabad!' was written in brick red colour on the wall. When he passed the women's restroom, it smelt of women totally. The noise which he heard inside resembled that of the screeching sounds made by birds when their nests are destroyed. In the bathroom a long figure was drawn and management written on top of it. In pencil, the private parts of one Jayalakshmi were drawn ... Guru felt shy.

He came back to his place. The plate was ready to strike for rivetting. He had left his job card on the supervisor's table before leaving. If a rivet was struck in three seconds, the worker received just his salary. If a rivet was struck in two seconds, three rupees, and one per second would get five rupees as incentive. It was humanly impossible to do one per second! After three o'clock, you would get chest pain.

Guru started hitting the rivet. Tatak tak tatak tak tatak tak tatak tak tatak tak………… the work was simple and easy. Place the plate with the left hand, step on it with a leg, give, tread, give, tread, give, tread…..

It was at this precise moment that his headache became unbearable and he felt dizzy for a slightly longer time than usual. He stopped working and stared with unseeing eyes. He saw a yellow dot hanging midway in front of the girl's chest who was far away. It looked like the yellow of an egg. He heard a whirring noise in his ears! I should not have come to the factory today, should have stayed at home.

He seemed to have felt better a little later. He started operating the machine again. He heard the whirring noise again after thirty seconds and he stopped the machine. He could feel the headache very clearly. He walked to the dispensary after getting the supervisor's permission.

The dispensary was neat and clean. The steel chairs were vacant and waiting for patients and it smelt of medicines. Behind the glass partition was the restroom. The medical officer had a separate cabin. The Malayalee nurse behind the small square window counter was also in the family way. She looked at Guru Prasad and asked his name.

"Guru Prasad."

"Staff number?"

"17163."

"Section?"

"Assembly."

"What is the problem?"

"Headache."

Before he could complete the sentence, she gave him a pink coloured tablet and water in a plastic glass. Guru looked at all the giant sized bottles there. He could read the names written on them. Things were a little clearer. They were hazy a little earlier. He thanked her, swallowed the tablet and returned to the section. The union office was on his way back to the factory. Eight people were sitting and talking on a bench inside. Guru wondered whether they had any duty at all. He could see dried black ink on the table. There were many glue bottles. A Godrej cupboard could be seen. Both national and international political leaders photos adorned the walls. Guru stopped and peeped through the curtain.

"What is it?"

Guru thought for a moment. Let me find out whether these people can help me in some way.

"I have to receive NLTC arrears. They have not been released by the accounts department since the last three months. They just keep on dragging it."

"What is your name?"

"Guru Prasad."

"Staff number?"

"17163."

"Are you a member of our union or theirs?"

Guru thought for a moment. He was not a member of either union. He mumbled, "Ours only."

"Have you paid your subscription?"

"No one asked me!"

Immediately, the union member's face turned red and he flared up in anger. "Will anyone come and ask for your subscription? Don't you have a responsibililty to pay your subscription. Has not the union sacrificed many things for you people? Have not the leaders gone to prison for your sake?"

Guru didn't have any answer.

"How did you get your arrears last month? Who got your CDS instalment? What about your production bonus? First pay your subscription."

Guru replied, "I don't have change."

"You scoundrel! Have we to run around like dogs and fight to get your LTC? You wretch! Run! Run away from here! We get people like you also!"

Guruprasad said softly, and at the same time with slight anger in his voice,"Hey you!" In the meanwhile, a thin man who was present there said, "Ustad, he is their man." The man pushed him away by keeping his hand lightly on the nape of Guru's neck. Guru staggered and looked back at them after going some distance.

All the eight people were laughing in mockery. The man who pushed him was an assistant leader, Krishnaiyya.

Guru knew him by name. He would be standing right in front in all the agitations. Guru felt like crying because of the insult meted out to him. He was angry. He regretted coming to them for their help. He walked away from there abusing them as 'guttersnipes' in his mind. He came back to his seat. "Rivet, rivet, rivet...."

The coffee break was at four-thirty in the evening. By ten past four everybody was ready with their tumblers for coffee. Guru was still striking the rivet in disgust after the morning's events. Srinivasamurthy, who was standing next to him said, "Let's go, don't toil so much for the company." Srinivasamurthy's tumbler was shining. He had put a ring around it and kept it in a grand condition by etching his name, Srinivasamurthy, Staff no. 16187 on it. He had milk everyday by producing a false medical certificate citing health reasons. There was a rumour going around that he and Angelmary who was working eight benches away were in an illicit relationship. Srinivasamurthy was an active union worker. He wore only silk shirts. He worked for two hours at a stretch, but still managed to get the full incentive. He has many people to do his bidding. He is an important assistant leader among the working class geneology. He is the right hand man of Krishnaiyya. Both Krishnaiyya and Srinivasamurthy are always seen together. Once they both misbehaved with a dancer during a floor show in Omarkhayyam restaurant and returned home after being beaten black and blue and with swollen lips. Four enquries were slapped against Krishnaiyya. He had threatened the enquiry officers.

He had threatened that he was not responsible if the enquiring officers met with accidents in case of an adverse judgement. Though Krishnaiyya is a lean man, he has control over many rowdy henchmen. He doesn't know anything about union tenets or Marxism, or trade union movements. His weapons are only bashing up people, kicking a row and abusing in filthy language. Speech was another weapon.

At six in the evening, Srinivasamurthy asked Guru Prasad what was wrong with him. He replied that he had a headache. Srinivasamurthy suggested that he work a half shift and go back home. The OT buses came by seven. Guru replied, "It is ok. I can manage."

By quarter to seven in the evening, the factory looked different as a result of different sounds and different lights. Guru just sat down. His blood pressure was very high. Some blood vessels in his brain burst and blood oozed slowly in his head. Darkness fell before his eyes. Srinivasamurthy noticed Guru staring with unseeing eyes.

Many blood vessels burst in many places in Guru's brain. Haemorrhage! Small blood streams mingled with the fluid in which the brain was floating. Cells were destroyed. The bubbling blood attacked his senses and he lost consciousness. He just slipped down near the machine itself.

Srinivasamurthy rushed and caught hold of him, calling out, " Guru, Guru, look at me."

Guru could hear, "Guru, Guru," before losing consciousness. He wanted to answer. He wanted to say, "Saraswathy, Prasanna," but slid down unable to speak. Both Srinivasamurthy and Dominique held him. They lifted him up in an awkward position—one lifted his head, another his leg, a third his armpits and his sides. Everybody started giving their advice.

Somebody suggested sprinkling water on his face. Another suggested to make him sit.

The dispensary was just a stone's throw from the factory. Somebody rang the dispensary and gave the message in the following manner:

"Is it Gangappa?"

"Yes"

"Namaskaram, are you in good health?"

"Namaskaram, what do you want?"

"A man has fainted here."

"What does 'here' mean?"

"In 3.2 building, close to the main shop."

"Faint?"

"Yes."

"Then you do one thing. You contact 8866 directly. They will send an ambulance."

"What is 8866?"

"The main hospital."

"Will there be an ambulance?"

"Yes."

"8866?"

"Yes."

"Will there be a doctor?"

"The doctor may not be there but when called will come

from the colony."

"Repeat the number 88…"

"66."

"66.Thanks, bye!"

He put down the telephone. Just in front of the telephone it was written in block letters and very clearly. "For emergency medical help, contact 8866."

8866 was contacted.

"Who is the patient?"

"Guru Prasad."

"Staff number?"

"Not known. I'll tell you when you come here. An ambulance is needed immediately."

"Where?"

"Machine shop, 3.2 building."

"Ok."

It was the time for change of duty for the ambulance driver. Hence, it was better to leave as soon as his relief came otherwise he would miss the shift bus.

The relief came after fifteen minutes. During that time, another three cells got damaged in Guru's brain. His faculty to move his hands and legs got affected very severely.

As soon as the ambulance came, they laid Guru inside the vehicle. His friends, both Srinivasamurthy and Dominique also got into the ambulance.

The ambulance, with the sirens blaring, zoomed to the

factory hospital which was very close by. A man went inside to get a stretcher. Guru was transferred to the stretcher and then to a trolley. A nurse checked his pulse which was racing. She opened his eyes and saw the pupils sunk deep into the eyes. She picked up the phone and called Dr Rajalakshmi.

Generally speaking, no doctor stayed in this hospital after six in the evening. They went back home. The duty doctor can go back home. But they have to be prepared to attend to any emergency. Today, it was Dr Rajalakshmi's duty.

Rajalakshmi was about fifty years old. She has two daughters and a son and has put in twenty years of service. Her husband abandoned her and their children. When she was young, she married for love, out of caste, left all her near and dear ones, gave birth to her children in quick succession, lost her hair considerably, put on weight and when she was almost the size of a barrel, she discovered that her husband had an illicit relationship with the maid servant. That too, in a shocking and surprising manner. On their wedding anniversary, she went shopping with the children and returned home to collect her purse which she had forgotten only to see her husband in a compromising position with the servant in their own bedroom and on their bed. The disgust which Rajalakshmi felt at that sight left a deep scar for the rest of her life. The wound never healed. Whenever she thought about it, the wound started bleeding. She didn't speak to her husband, not a single word, not even a single syllable after the incident. One day, her husband spent all his money and started drinking. She didn't bother. He came home at odd hours, she never questioned him. He suffered from cirrhosis, she did not sympathize with him. One day, he disappeared all of a sudden. She didn't make a complaint to the police.

Everybody calls her Dr Raji. It is eight years since her husband left her but there is no change either in her lifestyle or the way she dresses—the same bindi, the same hairstyle, the same face, the same colourful saris, nothing has changed. Both her daughters have grown taller and are studying. There is a telephone at home.

When the telephone rang, Dr Raji was preparing food for her children at home. Her daughters had gone to spend time with their college friends in the neighbourhood.

She removed the pressure cooker, picked up the telephone and said, "Hello."

"Doctor, I'm the duty nurse on the line. There's a patient here. He is unconscious but his pulse can be felt. He has no temperature."

"Vomiting?"

"Just a minute ... Did he vomit? No, he didn't vomit."

"Did he eat anything?"

"No, he had only coffee. Can I send the vehicle?"

"Who is the driver?"

"Kadar Pasha."

"Ok. Send the vehicle."

Dr Rajalakshmi removed the boiled rice and the pressure cooker from the gas stove. She released the pressure slowly and opened the cooker from which the steam was released in a jet. She took out the vegetables and meat pieces from it and cooked them with the freshly made gravy in the frying pan. ... The ambulance reached her house, sounded the horn and rang the bell. She said, "one minute" through the window ... added the aromatic spices, finished making the curry, left curd, papad etc. on the table, properly covered. She went to the front room, changed into a fresh sari and left for the hospital.

Srinivasamurthy looked at the Malayalee nurse.

Guru, who was lying on the stretcher, had suffered irreparable damage to the brain cells due to haemorrhage.

Srinivasamurthy asked her, "Are you a union member?"

She answered indifferently, "No". She was healthy. Her starched white uniform had big buttons and he could see her lingerie under the uniform. He looked at her waistline.

"Who is the doctor?"

"Dr Rajamma."

"Mrs Raji?"

"Yes."

"Oh!" He looked at the clock.

He had had a difference of opinion with Dr Raji and had heated arguments with her earlier. She refused to sign one of his leave letters and give a medical certificate. Once she refused to prescribe a tonic and accept a private doctor's certificate. She asked for a review and then certified that there was nothing wrong with his health. This resulted in the management cutting his salary for eight days.

Srinivasamurthy looked at his watch again and said loudly to Dominique, "Slut, the ambulance was sent about half-an-hour earlier and she has not yet come."

"Who, brother?"

"Oh! She, Dr Raji! They are all paid a salary and retained. She should be sacked. Irresponsible wretch!"

The nurse was writing in a big ledger and ignored them.

Dr Rajalakshmi asked the ambulance to take an adjacent street. Both her daughters were listening to pop music. Raji stopped in front of the house and managed to get the door opened despite the band's loud music. She entrusted the house keys to her daughters. This took about five minutes.

Srinivasamurthy picked up the hospital telephone and rang the factory. "Hello, Sesha? Krishnaiyya is in the union office. Call him for a minute."

As Srinivasamurthy was waiting by the telephone, Dr Rajalakshmi arrived. Immediately, she went to the room where Guru was lying. She checked the pulse. She examined him with a stethoscope. She realized that the heart beat was faster than normal. The whole face was flushed. She flashed the torch in his eyes.

Srinivasamurthy was standing next to the telephone just across and Dominique was with him.

She asked, "Who brought the patient?"

Dominique said, "I brought him."

"How long has he been unconscious?"

"He was alright till the evening coffee time. After the coffee, he was not fully alright. He is unconscious since the last half-an-hour."

Rajalakshmi was alone with Guru Prasad and she wheeled in a temporary screen. The three cases of loss of consciousness, which she had ever attended to, had all related to food poisoning. Now also they were saying that Guru had fainted after his coffee. She herself had seen many foreign bodies floating in the canteen coffee. Dr Raji thought to herself it was better to consult Dr Raman. Was it not better if two people examined a case!

Srinivasamurthy was waiting for Krishnaiyya to come on the line. "Who are you?" she asked him.

He said roughly, "Staff."

"Hospital?"

"No, factory."

"Then why do you block the telephone? It is an emergency phone. It is not meant for gossiping. Give me the phone!"

Dr Raji snatched the phone from him and dialled Dr Raman.

Dr Raman was in bed with his wife. When the phone rang, he got out of bed and his wife grumbled.

"Hello".

"Dr Raman, Dr Rajalakshmi here."

"Yes?"

"I have to consult you in connection with a case. Can you come?"

"But I am not on duty."

"Yes, I know I am on duty. Even then, can you come for a second opinion."

"Can you tell me the case?"

"It seems to be a case of food poisoning. The patient is unconscious."

"What about the pulse?"

"Pulse can be felt."

His wife said, "Why don't you come here?"

"If it is food poisoning, refer him to ESI hospital. Doctor, is he a worker?"

"Yes, but I'm not sure this is a case of food poisoning."

"The symptoms point to food poisoning only. Our hospital is not equipped to deal with such an emergency. Just send him to ESI hospital. Is there an ambulance?"

"Yes, it is available."

"Just send him."

Dr Raman disconnected the telephone and continued what he was doing earlier.

When Raji put the phone down, she noticed that Srinivasamurthy was looking at her with hatred in his eyes. She went to Guru and examined him with the stethoscope. The heart beat was racing.

"Nurse, take out an ESI form."

Srinivasamurthy came near her. He might have heard the word ESI.

"Doctor, are you not admitting him?"

"This case has to go to ESI Hospital."

"Suppose he dies before that?"

"Look here man, I am the doctor. I know when to admit someone and when to refer him to ESI. Now don't stand in the way and trouble me. Pasha, come here."

Srinivasamurthy became angry and mumbled, "Is this the way to treat a worker? Slut! Just see how she is talking."

Dr Rajalakshmi was furious. "Mr! Don't you have a mother or sisters?"

"I have everybody. Thank God, they don't come to take treatment from you!"

Dr Raji felt like crying. As she was wearing spectacles, it was easy for her to control the tears which threatened to fall, by blinking her eyes. It is my destiny. A husband who is good for nothing. Now I have to take abuse from each and every sundry person just for survival.

She wrote a note.

'To the duty doctor. Attend to the food poisoning patient immediately who is referred to your hospital.' She signed the form, called the ambulance driver Kadar Pasha. "Take this patient to ESI and leave him in the OPD. Return only after giving this chit to them."

"Have I to return after leaving the patient there?"

"Yes."

"Come Guru, I am also coming with you," so saying

Srinivasamurthy also got into the ambulance. Guru Prasad was transported to the ambulance. Now the haemorrhage was spreading all through the brain happily. He was losing many more faculties in his unconscious state.

Dr Raji sat in the front seat of the ambulance. She asked the driver to drop her home on the way to ESI.

Srinivasamurthy thought angrily. 'See how arrogant she is. A man is critical. Can't she walk home? Will she wear away by walking? Or else is this old woman scared that she will be molested on her way back to her house?'

The ambulance moved slowly. The railway crossing gate was closed just as they reached there.

He said in exasperation, "We could have avoided the delay of the closed railway gate if only we did not go to the doctor's house."

Guru Prasad was in a deep coma. He didn't hear Srinivasamurthy's furious mutterings.

The ambulance stopped in front of ESI hospital's Casualty. The driver took the chit and gave it to the man in khaki uniform. Srinivasamurthy accompanied him.

The chit was shown to the duty doctor. The doctor, who was engaged in an interesting conversation with his female colleague saw the chit and said, "Poisoning case. We don't treat such cases. Take him to Victoria hospital."

Srinivasamurthy said, "Doctor, this is not poisoning but food poisoning."

"That's okay, but all the poisoning cases involve the police.

ESI does not touch these cases."

"So you won't admit him?"

"Positively not. These are our rules."

"Don't you people have any humane feelings?"

"Hey, you have come to the wrong hospital. Stop getting angry with me! You should have gone straight to Victoria Hospital."

"They only sent us here."

" Who?"

" The factory doctor."

"Has the factory doctor no sense? Have they to send poisoning cases to ESI hospital? Even now it is not too late. Rush the patient to Victoria hospital and they will attend to him immediately. Hurry up."

The doctor went inside. The lady doctor also went inside after a few moments.

Srinivasamurthy came outside.

The driver asked, "Where to?"

"Where else? Victoria Hospital!"

"I don't have permission. The doctor asked me to take him only up to ESI hospital."

"Look man! Did you see the patient? He is in a deep unconscious state."

"I have seen not only this man but a hundred cases like this. I am tired of driving the ambulance. My duty is very clear. If it is ESI, it is ESI only."

"Hey, you! Will you take him to the hospital or not? Do you

want me to make you lose your job?"

"You! Even if your grandfather comes, it cannot be done. Bastard!"

"What did you say?"

"I said bastard. You are a big bastard."

Srinivasamurthy said, "You are the bastard," and caught hold of the driver's collar.

The Muslim Kadar Pasha had a mercurial temper and was not the one to leave an uninvited fight.

He dragged Srinivasamurthy to the road outside the hospital and thrashed him mercilessly. Srinivasamurthy's attempts to hit him back were all in vain. Some people separated them in the dark while others watched the fight in mute silence.

Guru Prasad had just the heart beat and faint breathing alone left in his body.

Srinivasamurthy said, "If you have any honour, remain where you are. I'll be back soon." He went to his friend's house in Rajaji Nagar.

The driver drove the ambulance back to the factory hospital. He was speaking to himself while driving back to the dispensary. "Duty means duty only. Give in writing to go to Victoria and I'll go. Give me clear instructions and I'll follow them to the letter." Guru, who was shaking due to the movement of the ambulance did not hear these words of the driver.

As soon as he reached the hospital, the nurse asked him sleepily, "Have you left the patient?"

"No, ESI refused to admit the patient. They asked me to take him to Victoria Hospital."

"Why did you not go to Victoria?"

"Nobody told me to."

"What? Don't you know this much? Do you expect somebody to tell you all this?"

"Look here sister, you just mind your own duty. As it is, I have already had a fight. An arrogant fellow ordered me as if he owned the vehicle. Are you people going to answer if I receive a charge sheet from CMO for having taken the vehicle to Victoria? I have already been charge sheeted once because the ambulance was taken just a furlong from Gokulam."

"But this is an entirely different matter, Kadar. For this nobody would have said anything to you... okay ... okay, why have an argument with you?" She picked up the phone and called Dr Rajalakshmi.

"What? Is he not admitted?"

"No doctor! The patient was asked to be taken to Victoria Hospital and the driver brought him back saying that he has not got clear instructions on this point."

"How stupid! Ask him to rush the patient to Victoria immediately."

"One minute."

The nurse covered the mouthpiece of the telephone and said, "Doctor says you go to Victoria."

Kadar Pasha said, "Wait, I will talk to her myself."

"Hello, Kadar here. Yes Madam, what is it?"

"Kadar, take the patient to Victoria immediately and take the duty orderly with you."

"Yes Madam, am I not right in saying that I cannot take the vehicle without the doctor's permission?"

"Ok! Ok! Hurry up and leave immediately."

"ESI refused to take the case saying it is a poison case."

"That matter is over! Leave immediately."

"Then it is alright. Doctor has given permission. The doctor asked the duty orderly to come with me."

"He has gone for his dinner. He will be back in five minutes."

"Why five minutes? I'll wait as long as needed."

Srinivasamurthy was angry for the thrashings which he received from Kadar Pasha and went looking for his friends only to realize they had gone to see a film. Hence, he went to Hosahalli and met Krishnaiyya.

Dr Sadasiva Rao exclaimed and said, "Who said this is food poisoning?" When Guru Prasad was brought to Victoria Hospital Casualty, he was sent to Ward No 5. From there he was sent to the Intensive Care Unit where he was put on oxygen. The Duty doctor examined him and immediately called his superior, Dr Sadasiva Rao.

Dr Rao asked, "What is your name?"

"Somasekar."

"Have you done an L P? Lumbar Puncture?

"Yes Doctor, I've done it."

"Do an L P. Cerebral haemorrhage will be confirmed."

"Look at the blood pressure. How high it is! Look at his eyes."

"How long has this man been unconscious?"

"Probably four to five hours."

"What were you people doing till then? Why did you not bring him earlier?"

"First we went to ESI. They refused to admit him."

By now Dr Somasekar had turned Guru to his side, applied tincture on his back and pricked with a ten cm needle between the third and the fourth vertebrae, removed the injection syringe and left the needle in the gap.

A pale white liquid dripped. A few moments later a few blood clots could be seen.

"Doctor, see this!"

Sadasiva Rao exclaimed after seeing the blood clots, "I am right. Cerebral haemorrhage! He is in a very deep coma!" He opened the eyelids and examined him.

"Who is the factory doctor who has signed this?"

"Lady doctor, Dr Raji."

"Is she a gynecologist?"

"No! general practitioner."

Sadasiva Rao said to Somasekar, "Factory doctors are not experienced people. She has written food poisoning."

"How did you know that it was a cere-breach?"

"History, young man, history! Blood pressure has shot up and all the vessels are breached and blood has oozed all over the brain.

All the brain cells might have got damaged." Dr Rao shook his head. "Food poisoning! Bloody shit! If only the BP was checked, it would have been known within a minute."

"What is the treatment for him now, doctor?"

"For him? He is a dead man, just a breathing machine!"

"Could he have been saved?"

"Had he been brought five hours earlier, he could have been saved. The moment he said he was feeling dizzy and feeling faint, he should have been brought immediately. By giving an overdose of anti-hypertensive drugs, he might have been saved. Anyhow, put him on the drip. By the way, where are his relatives? Have they been informed?"

"I don't know, Sir!"

"Are there no welfare officers in the factory?"

In the meantime, both Srinivasamurthy and Krishnaiyya entered in a great hurry. Krishnaiyya gave a half salute to the doctor. His eyes were blurred. He had come leaving his drinking halfway. Srinivasammurthy looked at the driver and said, "This is the fellow, Krishna."

Krishaniyya said, "Wait, we can deal with him later." He turned to the doctor and asked, "Will the man be saved?"

"It is very difficult. We can't say anything. Are you the factory welfare officer?"

"No, I am a union member."

"This man should have been brought five hours earlier. The diagnosis of food poisoning is completely wrong. The patient suffered cerebral haemorrhage. Probably, he has a history of high blood pressure. His card would have revealed this. Besides, no doctor seems to have checked his BP. Had it been checked, he could have been cured by giving BP medicines. Now he is more or less, a lost case.... He may be breathing for two or three days, that's all."

Krishnaiyya's face hardened. Srinivasamurthy said, "How about this Krishna?"

Krishnaiyya looked at Guru Prasad who was lying with his eyes closed, breathing peacefully with a tube inserted into his nostrils. Glucose was flowing in from the left side. The face looked familiar.

"Oh my god! He was at the union office this afternoon. He mentioned something about LTC arrears. I promised to do the needful. *Chi Chi*! Bastards! Shameless scoundrels. Are you people running a hospital? Murthy, it will be decided one way or the other tomorrow. Either I die or the hospital is burned down. I swear to do this."

"What about this driver?"

"We can burn him also tomorrow."

"First, his family is to be informed."

"Krishna, his wife is in the family way."

"Even then, we have to inform her. Do you know where he lives?"

"Yes, I know."

"No sleep tonight ... Should have announced at the 3 o'clock essential shift itself." They came out of the hospital very quickly.

Krishnaiyya bought two packets of Charminar.

"What is his name?"

"Guru Prasad."

"Guru! Comrade Guru!"

At twelve in the night, the doorbell rang incessantly. Saraswathy, who was sleeping, woke up with a start. Without opening the door, she asked, "Who is at the door?"

"It is me, Srinivasamurthy."

Which Srinivasamurthy? Should I open the door or not?

"Sister don't be scared .... I am Guru's friend Srinivasamurthy ... Vatsala's husband!"

"Oh!"

She opened the door. Two people were standing outside. Srinivasamurthy's face looked familiar.

"Sister don't be panicky...."

"Has anything happened to him?"

"He is slightly unconscious... he is in the hospital."

"Please get into the taxi."

When Saraswathy came to the ward, it was one in the night. Guru Prasad was lying very quietly. Thank God! I thought it was some accident. He is lying so peacefully. There was no facial movement. Breathing was normal. They had removed his oxygen mask also.

She called him and very slightly tapped his cheeks. His head tilted from side to side. She kept her hand on his chest. The heartbeat was normal. The body was warm.

Oh! Nothing. Just a simple state of unconsciousness. Tomorrow morning, everything would be alright. He would wake up in the morning. Thank God! I panicked thinking it was something very, very serious. Only *Tirupati Perumal* has saved him. The face is calm. There is no danger.

The human brain has many astounding features. One of the wonders is that God has placed the centre for regulating breathing and the heart beat at the deepest, innermost centre of the brain.

Guru Prasad's whole brain was damaged due to haemorrhage, except for this part. Hence his breathing and heart beat, both were normal. But for how many more days or hours, was the question!

A new day was born.

Administration manager, Rajaratnam, paid his obeisance to different gods like Saibaba,Ram, Goddess of Mangadu , Ashta Lakshmi, Guruvayur Krishnan, whose pictures were hung all over his puja room. Then he smeared his forehead with the sacred ash and left for the factory. He prayed to God that today also everything should go well like every day as he walked towards the factory. Rajaratnam didn't drink coffee. He was scared that those who worked in the Personnel Department would get ulcers if they had coffee. He used to get special milk from the canteen. He had put in fifteen years of service. He was a very experienced man. He was an expert in handling strikes, lock-outs, charge-sheets and pensions. He managed to get everything done by talking to the union people. He never sought police help.

The moment Rajaratnam entered the factory hall, he had

the premonition that something had gone seriously wrong. By now, all the factory workers should be in their respective shops. Instead, they were all talking to each other in small groups. The security officer approached him and said, "Sir, please enter the office through the rear entrance."

But the others saw him and burst into a slogan:

"We want…"

"Justice!"

"We Want..."

"Justice!"

Rajaratnam entered the register section in a trice, crossed the chairs, reached the staircase through the inside path and entered his cabin. The moment he saw the crowd, he realized that there would definitely be pelting of stones. Outside, the commotion increased. He locked his cabin from inside and closed all the windows. The moment he sat down, the internal telephone buzzed. His PA said, "Sir, the union leader wants to meet you."

"Which union?"

"Both the unions."

"Oh! Have they joined together? Tell them to wait for fifteen minutes. First call the security officer."

The refusal to meet the leaders immediately increased the pitch of slogan shouting. Krishnaiyya stood on a stool right in the middle of the shops, in the open space and was speaking. "Friends, if only you know how our dear friend, comrade and our own blood, Guru Prasad was treated by the factory's hospital, your blood will boil. The doctor sends him to ESI hospital by wrongly diagnosing it as food poisoning. … Comrades! Do you know what the doctor did before the ambulance left? When our comrade Guru was unconscious and fighting for his life, this old lady doctor with lipstick gets dropped at home and then only sends the ambulance to the hospital. Do you know what happened in ESI? How was your colleague and co-worker treated there……?"

Krishnaiyya was talking loudly, shaking his hands and legs. Slowly, one by one, the workers came out of their shops and listened to him with rapt attention.

"Who is Guru Prasad?"

"He is at the machine assembly shop. A very fair boy with a squint in his eyes. He was always with Srinivasamurthy."

"Is he dead?"

"That's what they say... If the hospital touches you, they won't leave you till you are dead."

"His wife is in an advanced state of pregnancy. The poor thing!"

"They were married only last year … this is their first child."

Srinivasamurthy, with seven or eight of his cronies, entered into each and every branch of the factory which was spread over acres and acres of land, and ordered the workers to come out. A worker was dying in the hospital due to wrong medication. Why bother about work? …. Everybody come out…!

Slowly, the crowd was swelling in front of Rajaratnam's office. His telephone was ringing non-stop.

The director from the head office contacted him. "What is this? Why are all the workers outside making trouble?"

"Sir, there was some problem when a worker was admitted to the hospital last night."

"Is the agitation for such a simple matter? What is the worker's name?"

"Sir, it is Guru Prasad. He is a mechanic in the assembly section."

"Is he in our factory hospital?"

"No, he is in Victoria."

"What can we do about that?"

"It seems that there was a delay in getting him admitted there."

"Is there no procedure? Is there a strike for that? If there is no production for a day, do you know the loss to the factory? Do something man!... Just promise them that he will be transferred to the best nursing home in the city to be treated and see to it that they return to work."

"Yes sir."

The moment Rajaratnam put down the phone, it rang again.

He picked it up. "Sir, union people. They are asking, 'Will he give permission or shall we enter by breaking the door?' They threw ink on me from the inkpot."

"Ok, ok… send them in."

Rajagopal, Sami, Krishnaiyya, Robert, Karunakaran! My goodness! Everybody at the same time? INTUC, AITUC, everybody. Rajaratnam finally prayed to Lord Murugan.

Rajagopal was a very haughty man, sporting an awe inspiring moustache. He was tall and well built. He slapped a paper on the table and said, "Are you aware of the problem?"

"Yes, I know. You people make a lot of fuss for a very simple matter. Now what do you want? You want the best treatment for Guru Prasad? Is that not so? Just now the director rang up and said that he can be admitted in any nursing home of your choice at the company's expense."

"Sir, but by then the man will be dead and gone."

"Who says so? Don't spread any rumours. Just now I rang up the Dean of Victoria Hospital. He is alive positively."

"Alive means ... laughing and talking?"

"No, he is unconscious."

"Do you know why he is unconscious? It is because of the useless treatment given by the useless doctors in your useless hospital. Do you know what happened last night, Mr Rajaratnam?"

"Yes, I know. We can hold a proper enquiry. Do you know what is the most important thing before that? All of you have to go back to work peacefully. Ask each and every worker to return to his job. We can hold talks later."

"Won't you even glance at the paper? These are the four conditions for us to return to work."

Rajaratnam read the paper:

Remove the killer, Dr Rajalakshmi from service.

Ask the CMO to proceed on leave

Formulate an impartial committee to look into the working of the hospital.

Punish the driver Kadar Pasha.

The talk, across the table, can take place only if these four demands are met with immediate effect.

Rajaratnam said, "First you have to go back to work. Then only I will look at this paper."

"No."

"In that case, half a day's salary of all those who came out of the factory will be cut."

Rajagopal laughed.

"Do you want me to put a fifth condition, Mr Rajaratnam? You have to resign your post. Is that okay with you?"

"You can put in as many conditions as you want."

"Let's go. This man is like a brick wall." They all went outside.

Rajaratnam was perspiring. At the very beginning itself, you should not give in. This would set a wrong precedent. Stupid lady. How many problems created due to negligent work. Again the director called him on the phone.

"Have they returned to work?"

"No Sir. They are demanding umpteen things. They are very adamant."

"Have you informed the police?"

"Yes, it is time for them to arrive. But the situation is tense."

"What are their demands?"

"They want the lady doctor to be dismissed, the CMO to go

on leave, and an enquiry committee to be set up."

"Tell them that the lady doctor can be served a suspension notice."

"They won't agree, Sir."

"Call me if they don't return in half-an-hour's time."

"Yes, Sir."

Rajaratnam looked out of the window.

Rajagopal, Krishnaiyya and others were standing in the balcony and about five thousand agitated workers were standing below listening to them, shouting slogans.

"The slave of the management, the bastard Rajaratnam threatens to cut our salary. Tell me comrades, do you want your salary or comrade Guru Prasad's life?"

"We want life ... life." Five thousnd voices chorused in unison.

"Do we need money?"

"No... No."

"Let's march to the hospital! Let's burn that down."

Rajaratnam was startled by the noise made by broken glass. A chappal was thrown at the window. The glass broke in splinters. The other slipper which followed fell in the verandah.

He felt a chill in the spine as he saw the crowd moving towards the hospital. He rang the security officer.

"Have you informed the police?"

"Yes Sir, I have informed them. They should be here at any moment."

"You should have called them earlier, Nagaraj! Do you know

how much loss is to be incurred by the non-arrival of police now?"

"Everybody is going to the hospital, Sir."

"They will destroy the hospital before the police arrive."

"Is the man dead?"

"Who said so?"

"That's the rumour."

"First and foremost, kill that rumour. Tell them that he is not dead, but alive."

"Who is to tell them? They have caused a lot of damage inside the factory also. We have called the fire brigade to douse the fire in the moulding section."

"My god!"

Rajaratnam could feel the fear bubbling inside his body. The situation was moving beyond control. The police had not yet arrived. They had started torching things. The telephone tinkled. It had to be the director.

"Hello, have they returned to work or not?"

"No, not yet, Sir."

"I have spoken to the Victoria Hospital doctor to take good care of the man. Inform the workers about this also."

"They are not in a mood to listen to any of our words."

"Where are they?"

"Everybody has walked out of the factory and is moving towards the hospital."

"Is the factory empty?"

"Almost."

"Is this the way to run a factory? Do something and see to it that they return. Quick."

"Yes, Sir."

The moment the phone was put down, the security officer's call came through.

"It's all gone, Sir. They are destroying and breaking the hospital into pieces."

Krishnaiyya was intoxicated by the news of destruction. I am the leader. There are six thousand people at my beck and call. No, ten thousand people who would execute each and every command of mine. "If I say, pelt stones, they will pelt stones. If I say spit, they will spit fire."

The crowd was pouring a can of petrol on the hospital's front portion.

"We will fight till our last breath. We won't buckle under management's pressure and threats. Zindabad! Zindabad!"

Through the back door of the hospital, nurses in their white uniforms, orderlies and doctors ran to save their lives. Patients mingled with the crowd. Crackers meant for Diwali burst with a loud bang. The rose saplings were trampled upon. Thirty new born babies started crying simultaneously in the maternity ward.

"Mr Rajaratnam, this is the limit. Fire inside the factory! Outside, the hospital is badly damaged. As the administrative manager, you should have avoided the situation. You should not have allowed this to go to this extent."

"I am sorry sir,! It happened all of a sudden!"

"Do you think that such a situation arrives with an announcement? What do they want?"

"They want Dr Rajalakshmi to be dismissed."

"Ok, do that. Dismiss her."

"CMO Dr Balagopal has to proceed on leave."

"Ask him to go on leave. You agree to whatever their demands are. As long as they return to work, everything is okay."

"Excuse me. I felt that we should not give in so easily like cowards."

"Don't talk rubbish. Do you know the value of the machinery and other material in the factory? Twenty lakhs. Just tell them that the management is ready to send the worker to Jaslok Hospital. I can't manage any more."

"The police will arrive at any moment, Sir."

"Mr Rajaratnam! You do what I say. Within an hour, I want peace in the factory otherwise you will lose your job. Be careful. This is the last warning."

Two lorry loads of police with helmets arrived. They got down at the gate of the hospital. They plucked out like weeds the men who had pelted stones from the crowd. They caned them below the knees with their lathis and made them cry. One round of tear gas was used.

In less than five minutes, the place got cleared of the agitating workers. All of them ran helter-skelter. Irrespective of their age, they ran like young boys.

Rajaratnam called Rajagopal, Sami, Krishnaiyya, Robert and

Karunakaran to his cabin at eleven and gave them a letter.

'As discussed earlier in the morning, Dr Rajalakshmi will be dismissed from service. Dr Balagopal has been asked to proceed on leave. A committee comprising of three independent and impartial members will be formed to enquire into the factory and hospital workings. Driver Kadar Pasha will be transferred immediately to the establishment section. The workers are ordered to return to their respective workshops immediately.'

Signed, Ratnam, AM.

There was a discussion about changing the word "ordered" to "requested" for a few minutes.

To meet Comrade Guru Prasad in the hospital, buses were demanded. This demand was immediately approved by the management.

"Half-day salary?"

"On my word of honour, it will not be deducted."

Dr Rajalakshmi, since it was her off day, for a change, had left for her sister Chandra's place in Palace Orchard early morning .

"Chandra, I am holding on to a good, permanent job. My son has taken after his father. He is useless. If the girls study well and come up in life, I can continue in this job for another eight years. This will help me to repay all the loans and feel relieved."

"Raji, when do you expect your promotion? Did you not mention that you are the next deputy chief?"

She said, "It will come. I expect it very soon."

The factory became peaceful by the afternoon. Everybody

returned to their respective jobs.

Rajagopal laughed.

"He pissed. You should have seen his face. As if struck by the devil."

"Krishnaiyya, did they not agree to each and everyone of our demands?"

"Do you think a day's production such a small matter? What about the workers? The moment we ordered, did they not follow us without any questions?"

Krishnaiyya said, "Who did the talking?"

Srinivasamurthy said, "You people have forgotten me!"

"What will you have? Whisky?"

"Cheers, cheers."

"For worker's unity, they clinked their glasses. Chicken was brought.

The Accounts Officer, Ramakrishnan added up everything.

The total loss was sixteen lakh twenty thousand rupees, which included half-a-day's production, damaged goods and bus expenses. He called the director.

"Sir, Ramakrishnan here. The total loss is Rs 16.2 lakhs, Sir."

"Leave it. Thank god, the loss is only this much. Had we listened to Rajaratnam, the loss would have crossed a crore."

Grur Prasad died at 2.16 in the afternoon. His heart suffered fibrillation, like the flutter of a pigeon's wings. The ECE monitor attached to his body raised an alarm and made a beeping sound. The duty doctor rushed inside, thumped his chest, injected into his heart directly and tried his level best to revive him. But Guru breathed his last, failing to respond to any of these emergency treatments.

Saraswathy had gone to the next ward to fill the thermos with hot water.

The officers in the factory were extremely cautious and well prepared for any eventuality. Six buses were ready to transport the workers who wanted to visit Guru Prasad in the hospital.

'We regret the sad demise of our Comrade Guru Prasad' was written in bold letters and stuck on the notice board. Two truck loads of police kept vigil outside.

The six buses were filled to capacity by the workers. The buses left for the hospital. Half the people got down at Malleswaram. Some people got down at Majestic.

When the bus reached Victoria Hospital only five hundred workers could be seen. When they were walking along the long cobbled corridors, one of the them asked, "What is the name of the worker?"

"Who?"

"The one who died."

"Mohan Prasad."

"No, Murali Prasad."

"No, somebody said, Satyamurthy."

"Srinivasamurthy would know better."

"Where is Srinivasamurthy?"

"Some name, hurry up."

# Hey Raja, Stop

HEY RAJA, Stop!

"Does it matter if I lose cattle or land?

Does it matter if I lose near and dear ones?

Does it matter if I lose gold of highest purity? Oh parrot,

Just a semblance of a smile (from you) will suffice."

At least 'a semblance of a smile' was left for the poet who wrote the above couplet. But for me, everything was lost. How did it happen? Horse races? Gambling? Share market? No, nothing of that sort. Just a second, not even the time taken to crack a finger, and they said, I am not 'Me'!

Before the end of this story, I will kill that rascal for what he had done to me. But first, a few introductions. Just to clear your doubts. I am definitely not insane. Let's make that clear at the beginning itself. No need for any doubt at all.

Who am I?

I can answer you from different planes. From the Upanishads, 'Aham Brahmam.' But also I am a husband, a father, a hunter who holds secret desires. I am Jawahar Vittal, Company Director. I am a man, a Homosapien—How many different 'Me's'! What if I were to lose everything, in just a single second?

Am I not confusing you again?

I am Jawahar Vittal. My father was a true patriot but is no more. My father had just a hundred and fifty rupees in cash. When he died, I was just nineteen years old. A graduate. There were not many educated people, especially graduates in our community. Bhaktavatsalam supported me, married off his daughter (Bhuvaneshwari) to me and financed my business which expanded. The passing away of my uncle, birth of a daughter, the many fold expansion of business took place, and by my fortieth birthday, I became the business magnate of 'Deluxe Spare parts Industries' with a turnover of eighteen lakhs. The success story of my life taught me the moral, 'Marry a rich girl.'

Bhuvaneshwari cannot be called ugly. It is my good luck that she happens to be a good home maker, whose appearance is pleasing to the eyes. She is capable of producing lip smacking dishes. She has a big red dot on her forehead. She has two younger sisters. My life was based on a strong foundation of pleasure, happiness, contentment and wealth. I am definitely going to kill that rascal who destabilized the very foundation of my life. Wait and see!

*Chithirai* is the Tamil first month. On New Year's Day, the office is closed. But everyone in the office congregates to perform special pujas. As per tradition, after entering the income on the first page in the new ledger which was blessed at Palani temple with a round red dot, we used to have coffee and snacks like cake, and samosas. At the same time I used to announce the promotions in the office and also the bonus declared for that year. Everybody used to wish me. It was always a joyful and happy event. This had been taking place for the last ten years. It was the *Rahu kaal*—the inauspicious time between 9 and 10.30 AM. Hence, I went to the office early so that the function could be finished before nine itself. Chitra had taken the car as little Shobha was singing in the school. I hired a taxi to the office which was on Peter's Road. One way traffic. That is when the problem started.

I entered the office. Everybody used to wait for me at the entrance. Nobody was there. Has nobody come in as yet? But I could hear voices inside. Have they begun without me? I entered.

The puja was in progress . The tables were rearranged, lighted incense and broken coconut could be seen in front of Goddess Lakshmi's picture kept on the table. The ledger was decorated and sanctified. Everybody was standing around. He was standing in the centre smiling and talking to everybody. He was occupying my place. A complete stranger, smiling at telephonist Kalavati. Everybody was clapping. Who was he? Had he come to this office by mistake? He was giving a short speech.

" Dear friends! Our office is 11 years old this New Year's Day.

It started in a small shed but has expanded today with branches in Bangalore, Salem and Pudukottai."

He was mouthing my speech verbatim. I looked at him. He was almost my age. Had bushy side-burns. Very big head, much darker than me. I remembered the cowrie shell of Rameswaram. His teeth reminded me of that and he had a smile. Troublesome times! Deceitful eyes, slightly taller than me……

Shit! Who is he? Why do I compare myself with him repeatedly. First and foremost, I have to throw him out of this office. He keeps smiling at all my office girls. He is sitting on my chair in front of my table reading out the promotions and increment in the salaries conferred on the staff from the blue book.

"Did you not say stop?"

"I wanted to but somehow I was watching with great fascination. I don't know why, but I felt like standing, fascinated by the events."

"Telephonist Kala gets a raise of hundred rupees, a watch for Kandasami." He kept reading. Nobody even cast a glance at me. I wondered whether I had come to the wrong place. No, definitely not. This is my office, positively. There is a clock in the corner, a tube light, water cooler, my uncle's photo with a garland. My office definitely. Have they all ganged up together to make fun of me in my absence?

"Hmm…", I clucked. Everybody turned and looked at me.

I asked him, "Hey, who are you?"

At the same time he asked me, "Hey! Who are you?"

"Sir, at this point, I felt a bit confused. This place doesn't seem to be my office. I seemed to have come to a different place all of a sudden. It looks like a narrow lane. There is a slight trace of jack-fruit smell along with that of urine. It seemed to be a city connected with a temple. A young woman, about twenty years old, with a big bindi, danglers in her ears, lots of flowers in her hair, a chain with mango design as well as a single strand chain, who was neither sitting nor lying down but was in a half reclined position, with a semblance of a smile looks at me and says , 'Stop a moment, Raja.' Somehow I am reminded of this.

"Who is she?"

"I don't know. The single strand chain on her neck had a golden key! I distinctly remember that.'

" Then?"

"Then I came back."

"This is not a case of previous birth or any such thing. Mistaken identity? No. I felt that this was something much more serious. Those people who were surrounding him looked at me as if I was a complete stranger! This spurning surprised me. Had this been a practical joke the staff might have practiced for months together. This was definitely not a drama. What else could this be Sir?"

Swaminathan, my PA of eight years asked, "Whom do you want to speak to?" I had managed to get a Physical Training seat for his daughter.

"Swaminathan, what is all this rubbish?"

Swaminathan looked at the others with surprise writ large on his face. "Hey, he knows my name! How is it so?" Immediately, the man who was in the centre said, "Of course! Who are you?" Mani came near me and said, "Hello! This is an office. The entry is restricted. This is not a thoroughfare. Who let you in?"

"Who let me in? You cruel people! All of you have joined together and are acting a drama! Kala, don't you recognize me? Swaminathan! Hey Mani! Throw that man out! All of you have to be suspended for this action. Hey, you …. get lost!" I went closer to the table and grabbed his coat. He looked at the others and his face turned pale with fear. Mani said,"Hey, you! Don't dare to touch our boss."

"Ha! Boss! What a ridiculous thing to say!"

"Who is this man?"

"A mad man who wanders the streets."

" Probably due to the heat outside!"

"First and foremost, two of you catch him and throw him out! Why do you keep standing and staring? He has dared to touch our boss!"

"Call the police!"

"The people who dared not enter my room came and dragged me by the hand and threw me out into the street, Sir!"

What I felt at that time was neither shock nor confusion. A sudden fear! Something is wrong! Something doesn't seem to be right. There seems to be a missing link in the chain. Otherwise, my faithful staff would not dare to do this in their wildest dreams.

That too, Mani, Saminathan, Kala!

A crowd gathered in front of my office.

"What happened?"

"Some mad fellow. He came inside the office and attacked the boss."

"I am the boss!"

"Did you hear this?"

"Is he a dismissed worker?"

"No. A stranger."

"Sir, I am the company's Director! I am Jawahar Vittal. I am the owner. They all work under me."

"In Madurai, a man roams around the city calling himself Aringar Anna." (Aringar Anna—The founder of DMK, a strong political party of Tamil Nadu)

"Is he a drunkard?"

"No, it is the heat of the sun. *Chithirai* is the hottest period of summer. One or two people are afflicted like this in every street. Can't you feel the heat wave even at nine in the morning?"

Immediately, I needed a comfort zone in my mind to get some reassurance. I have done a Management Course. I have read thoroughly all Peter Drucker's books. I have not only studied but also know how to analyze and solve all the most difficult problems. I had never before experienced this sort of problem. I thought about it. I could not digest what had happened in the last half-an-hour. I am J Vittal. I am very sure of that. My wife will vouch for that. Unless I have been transformed into a big insect like Kafka's metamorphosis theory. Then it is a worrying matter. But that is pure fantasy.

"One minute Vittal! Why can't all this be fantasy?"

"Whatever I have narrated just now?"

"Yes!"

"Don't be funny! You will understand after you listen to me fully. Just pay attention without interfering in between. What is my problem? Why do my employees behave like this? How can all the fifty people be mad? It can't be. Are they doing this on purpose? If so, don't they know my temper? Won't I dismiss everybody? Or is it treason?"

It cannot be anything else but a betrayal of trust. Instigated and monitored by somebody. Something doesn't seem to click right. I am standing right in the middle of the street. There is no look of recognition on all the faces of the staff who stand at the gate of the office. If they are pretending, then it is superb acting. They could get a prize for their acting.

"Mani, Swami, Kala, Krishna, Veni! Don't you know me? Tell me. Don't you know who I am? I don't know what you hope to achieve by this madness. If it is a practical joke, please tell me. It is a different matter altogether whether I will forgive you. I am going to the police just now."

Laughter! "Oh! He is going to the police!"

"Hey buddy! How does he know all our names?"

"Yes of course! He is not mad. He has come here after hatching a plan. Hey you, how many of you are involved in this?"

"We ourselves can lodge a complaint."

"Make way. Boss is coming."

"Boss!"

"What is he saying?"

"He says that he is the boss. He wants to lodge a police complaint."

"Mister, are you this company's Director? Does this building belong to you?"

"Yes, of course!"

Laughter! A man laughed, joined by another, ten people, then a hundred laughed. The traffic in Peter's Road seemed to envelop the whole world in its laughter.

I told myself: "Vittal! Beware! Be careful. Keep quiet. You have to find out where the mistake is—whether in your mind or in the outer world. Only the law can protect you. Before that what you need is love and affection. Your wife's support and the bonding of your daughter.

Bhuvana, Shobha darling, Selvi, my house, my world, the roses in my garden, the shade of the mango tree and the gentle breeze of the neem tree.

I entered the house after paying off the taxi. I enter the house by opening the front gate. Julie barked at me furiously. Her chain is strained.....

"Julie....Julie....It is only me, dear...!"

"Who is there?"

"It is me, Bhuvana! Open the door." The door opened.

Bhuvana is standing and next to her is that rascal.....!

The worst possible torture a man can face is to see his wife with another man. That too, standing next to her, shoulder to shoulder. I am forty plus. Our age difference is seven years. She is still very pretty. She has been dependent on me each second of her life since she came into the house at a very young age, like a frightened young fawn. Her saris are chosen by me! She has seen only movies chosen by me. She came to me only when I nudged her. She has reaped the benefits of consent and cohabitation. But now she stands next to that rascal as if it is the normal thing to do. Her sari is slightly disarrayed. She rearranges it when her eyes fall on me. My whole body is raging with fire.

"Bhuvana, what is this? Who is that man?" My wife looks at me as if I am a complete stranger and then enquires, "Who is that?"

"Hey! Have you come here also? Kandasami, where has he gone.....?"

"Bhuvana, this man came to the office and created a ruckus there. It was very difficult to throw him out. Now he has come here also."

"Dear! Who is he? What does he want?"

"What? I am your husband!"

"Oh God! Why is he talking like this? I will go inside."

"In the office, he said he was the director. He comes here and says that he is your husband. How many different types of mad people are there. Bhuvana, you do one thing.....The police station number is written on the cardboard hanging above the telephone. Call them...."

"*Aiyyayyo*! I won't. I can feel a tremor running through my body."

"Hey, are you leaving or not?"

"Why should I leave my own house! It is you who has to go away."

At times, it seemed to be funny. "Where is Chitra?...Chitra...!"

Chitra enters. She is my wife's younger sister. A talented girl. She always gives me a pleasant smile. She has an appropriate smile for everything, be it the flower in the garden, the stars or a beggar. An easy and a pleasant smile.

"Chitra, come dear.....look at me. Is it not 'Me?' It is only 'Me' and 'Myself' alone. You tell these people clearly." I am almost on the verge of tears.

At the same time Shobha baby also comes there. My daughter! My own darling daughter! My genes! My chromosome! I have bathed her, powdered her, washed and cleaned her...my daughter! Now the tears start flowing down in streams! Grown ups—these people will tell lies. They may plot and conspire against me and say that it is not 'me'....but this child Shobha .....she can't tell lies. She has not yet learnt to speak untruths! She doesn't know how to tell lies. There is still a trace of godliness in her. You can't tell lies when you are five.

'Shobha dear, my darling! Dear you tell them who am I? Am I not your father? You always call me 'daddy, daddy!' Call me 'daddy' and prove that this man is a wretch to the police. Who am I? Who am I......tell Shobha...."

The child looks at me straight with wide eyes. Looks at Bhuvana and says,"Who is that uncle, mummy?"

I look at Chitra. She does not smile.

Gone! All that belonged to me gone! My identity is lost! I have lost myself. Everybody has joined together to say that I am not Jawahar Vittal! Then who am I?

"Kandasami, throw him out of the house!"

"Hey! Don't you dare touch me? I have known you since you were a small boy. You are a slave who grew up under my feet. Will you raise your hand and hit me?"

"Get lost, I say…."

The slave dog dragged me and threw me on the road.

I started screaming, having fallen on the road. "Hey, I am warning you all. This is not fair. A grave sin! None of you will do well! All of you will perish!"

About ten to fifteen people gathered in the street. Everybody was curious to know what was happening and enquired ….. "Sir, what happened? Has he not repaid a loan or some such thing?"

'No sir, he refuses to part with my wife and daughter."

"Who are you?"

"Varadan, don't you recognize me?"

"Can't recognise you. Who are you?"

"I am Jawahar Vittal! The owner of this house…..the master!"

"Oh! I see!"

"What do you mean by 'Oh! I see!'?"

"Hey Varadan! Why do you invite trouble?"

That was the final surgery, which cut me off completely. My office, my daughter, my near and dear ones, my street and my friends all joined together and said that I was not Jawahar Vittal. Why have all these things happened to me? Am I mad as they all profess? Am I really and truly mad? Does not this query, which I raise, itself prove that I am not mad? How can I be considered mad? I know each and every nook and corner of the house in front of me. I know each and every birth mark on my wife's body. I know each and every picture and book on the first floor of the house. I know how they are arranged also—*Criminal Justice*, *Fowler's Modern English*, *Naaladiyar*, *90 Minutes At Entebee*. I felt nauseated. I threw up on the pavement.

I thought deeply. Aah! I have realized how to solve the problem! How would I know so many details about the house had I been a stranger? Though they threatened to call the police they didn't do so—instead I would make a complaint against him with the police. Yes, I am going to prove my identity to the police. I decided to go to the police station.

"Did you not meet the girl afterwards?"

" Which girl?"

" That girl—that 'Stop Raja!' girl.

"Yes, I saw her! I saw her one night.... I will tell you that story later. Just now, the police. Is that okay?"

"You may get tired of my saying repeatedly that my memory is crystal clear. It may even irritate you. My aim is to prove the state of my mental faculty. I don't want you to come to the conclusion that I am insane. That is very important to me. That is all! Can you call a person insane simply because he doesn't understand a few things? Besides, can a mad person express all that happened in a coherent manner? In the police station there was a red fire extinguisher and a head constable's cycle. The cycle's wheel had a multi-coloured fluffy ring in the centre…The constable was very lean and looked undernourished. But his trouser which was starched, stood erect and firm. Am I not saying everything correctly?.....(laughter!) Don't laugh sir. Don't you understand how distressed I am to have to prove my sanity?"

The inspector looked up at me after a little while from the crime book.

"What do you want?"

"I want to make a complaint."

" Name?"

"Jawahar Vittal."

"Address?"

" 14,Thandavarayan Kovil Street!"

"Thandavarayan Kovil Street. Vadivelu, is that under our jurisdiction? Has it not been shifted to A-3?"

"No Sir, since March it is ours only." A voice from inside spoke.

" Yes Sir! What is the case? Theft or dacoity?"

" Both, and along with that, impersonation!"

"Impersonation?"

The inspector looked at me with a suspicious look. I have

met him before. Wait a minute. "Inspector, we have met before! Don't you remember? At the *Akhanda Bhajan* in Peter's Colony."

"May be. Tell me your case!"

I told him everything in great detail. The phone rang in between. He talked about two litres and three litres of kerosene. I spoke in length and in detail about what had happened. Finally, he stared at me and laughed.

"Why do you laugh?"

"What you say is that neither your wife nor your biological child recognized you."

"Yes."

"You want me to believe this?"

"That's what is happening! You can come and see for yourself! If everybody joins together and schemes against me, do I have any other option than to seek a remedy with the help of the police?"

"How is it possible? From what you say, you are the only one who speaks the truth and all others speak lies. Is it not so?"

"Yes Sir, precisely."

"How is that possible?"

"Everybody has schemed against me."

"A five-year-old child also?"

"That's what perplexes me."

"Why do they have to do this?"

"They are all taking revenge upon me in some way. Or else they have designs on my property and are behaving like this."

"What is the value of the property?"

"That's quite a lot."

"Do you think a small child would disown its father in favour of property?"

I said with irritation, "Then, why do they behave like this?"

"As far as I am concerned, I know just one thing. Instead of believing that the whole world is telling lies, it is easier to believe that you are the only one telling lies. So?"

"So?"

"Get lost and leave the place."

"Are you going to take my complaint or not?"

"Definitely….! Vadivelu, offer a seat to this gentleman and give him a sheet of paper. Get the complaint registered. Understood?"

Wait a minute! All of a sudden it struck me. *Chee Chee*! What a fool am I?

"Inspector! On the first floor of the house, a photograph of me and my wife is hanging on the wall. A colour photo, shot at GKVel's studio. I have a dark coat on and she is in a green silk sari….after seeing that, you can decide who is insane. I would have shown that as a proof but they won't let me inside the house! That's why I want to go with a police escort. Hope you have no objection to this."

The Inspector scratched his head pensively and called "Vadivelu" again.

Vadivelu's voice replied, "Let's go and check this."

I returned to my house again with a police escort around

noon. The sun was at its peak in the sky. The door was opened. That rascal again!

"What! Have you come again? Why are you so troublesome? Kandasami, Kandasami! Have you brought the police with you?"

The inspector said, "Sir, what is your name?"

"Jawahar Vittal."

I said, "I am Jawahar Vittal."

"Since this morning he has been troubling me."

"That is precisely my complaint also."

"Is that so! Wait. Madam, please excuse me for troubling you. Do you know this man?"

"I don't know him at all!"

I said in a piteous voice, "Bhuvaneshwari, why do you speak like this?"

"He says that there is a photo hanging upstairs."

"What photo?"

"Bhuvana, you go inside. What photo?"

"Inspector, you go inside and check whether the photo is there or not. I can wait outside. Then you can decide! I am not coming inside. This is my own house. Even then I am not coming inside."

"Sir, can I have a look at that photo just once? Is it hanging upstairs as he insists?"

" Yes,why not? By all means."

The Inspector said, "You wait here for a moment, I will be back soon." I said happily, "I'll wait here itself."

"Notice carefully. The staircase has eighteen steps. A carpet is spread on the floor. There is a mirror. It is hung with a tilt just above the door of the room."

"Ok, ok." As the Inspector went inside the house, I stood outside under the shade of the neem tree. The swing was moving in the gentle breeze. I remembered the time when I had bought this house from a retired forest officer after securing a loan. I remembered remodelling the house to make it more habitable with the help of carpenters, architects and masons. Tears welled up in my eyes. Why am I not able to establish my identity in my own house and enter it?

The Inspector came out of the house talking pleasantly with that rascal who was with him.

"Inspector, did you see?"

The Inspector smiled saying, "Yes, I have seen."

"Was the photo there?"

"Yes, it was there—chocolate brown coat, green silk sari. Everything was correct."

"Then what is the problem?"

"But the man in the photo is not you, but this gentleman."

"What? It cannot be. Inspector, you also scheme against me. He has bribed you too. Let me go and see." I ran inside. The Inspector stopped me and dragged me outside on the road.

"Sinners, Sinners." So saying, I sat down and wept piteously.

I am not the type to sit and weep in the middle of the road. Before this, I have faced many situations that threatened to ruin my life. In 1973, the company became almost bankrupt. Shobha was afflicted with jaundice and was saved by a hair's breadth. Then, I had a son who died when he was a year old.

These were the tragic occasions in my life. Even then I never wailed or lamented. Now I wept bitterly. When all my near and dear ones declare and vehemently swear that I am not who I say I am, I feel apprehensive. If I am not "me", then who am I?

*Chee Chee*! The question does not arise at all. Irrelevant question. I am definitely Jawahar Vittal. That Bhuvana's husband. Don't I know the mole on her breast? Don't I know the coin sized scar on her thigh? I am definitely Shobha's father! Don't I know Shobha since before her umbilical cord was cut? Everybody has ganged up together.

When they look at me, there is not even a slight trace of recognition! I have not looked at my face in the mirror since I woke up in the morning. Is it possible that my face has completely changed beyond recognition? Anyhow, let me check my face in a mirror.

"Bhuvana, get me a mirror from inside, please!"

The Inspector said, " I say, get lost!"

"Bhuvana! Look at his audacity to call her as if she belongs to him!"

"Shobha darling, you get a mirror from inside."

"No, I won't."

"Selvi….."

"Do you want to be pushed and thrown out again…..?"

"No need Sir, I will leave the place on my own. But…"

"No buts and ifs. Get lost I say….!"

I walked away in shock. Where to go? When they have deleted my name, address and identity, do I have a refuge? I just walked aimlessly. My eyes fell upon Muthu Deluxe Hair Dressers. I entered and sat upon the swivel chair and looked into the mirror. No, no change at all. The same familiar face of more than forty years, the same moustache. The same single strand of grey hair. I looked into the mirror and bared my teeth. The same teeth. The same gap between the teeth. The same gold filling on the tooth near the jaw. I opened my shirt and checked whether the mole on my shoulder was still there. No change at all!

"Sir, cutting...or shaving?"

"No! Can you check whether there is a black birthmark on my back just below the left shoulder?"

"You come into a hair-cutting salon to check whether there is a birthmark on your back! Go away. What a nuisance you are? Get up and get lost!"

I came out. What to do? Where to go? My first problem was to find a place to stay. I have many friends. I can go to anybody. State Bank Atma is a good friend. Suppose the same old story repeated itself?

"Hey Atma, I am Vittal."

"Excuse me…, but who are you? I don't seem to know you…" Somehow I felt that this is what would happen. There is some change in me! It is definitely not the face!...Then what is it?

Could it be like this? Do the others also perceive my face as seen by me? Or else does it look different to them? Let me check this.

Kala Photo Studio. Passport photo is developed and delivered in three hours. I enter and enquire. He asks for six rupees as advance. Thank God. There were two ten rupee notes in my pocket. What am I going to do for money now? He clicked my photograph with an old Rolifelx camera after seating me. He asked me to come after some time. I came outside the studio. I saw an Udipi restaurant just across the street. Many cycles were parked outside. There was a cinema hall on this side of the road. I went and sat inside. A Hindi movie. Amitabh Bachchan had no problems like me. Two heroines with big breasts. He romances both of them. Double role.

Has anybody given a double role to me also? The person whom I think to be 'myself' is not 'me.' He is a different 'me' altogether.

"I came outside, lighted a cigarette, splashed my face with water and wiped it thoroughly. There was a big textile shop opposite the theatre. Even during the day it had flashy lights. Many cars were parked under the tree. I am a regular customer of this shop. Very recently I had purchased a silk skirt for Shobha and saris for both Bhuvana and Selvi. I will go and just stand next to the shop keeper. Let me see whether he recognizes me. As I crossed the road to the other side, I saw her again."

"Who? Selvi?"

"Not Selvi. Sir! Selvi is my sister-in-law. I saw that girl, whom I told you about in the beginning—a nameless girl. I remembered the face. In some place, some house, on some cot."

"The one who said, 'Stop Raja'."

"Ah! yes, the same girl. I saw her. I saw her getting into the passenger seat of the car. She had a big parcel in her arms which she held to her chest tightly.

I called out "Hey! Hey!" She didn't turn. I clapped my hands. About forty people might have turned back to look at me. She also turned back and saw me. She recognized my face, looked straight at me and gave me a smile, got into the car and left.

I ran about ten steps after the car calling out, "Hey...! Hey...!"

"Did you note down the number of the car?"

"No. It didn't strike me to note the car number. Besides, what did the smile mean? Does it not imply that she knew me? But I do not know who she is. Don't know her name. Yet her face is deeply etched in my memory......I think she holds the key to my strange state of affairs! But she has flown away."

"Stop Raja?"

"Yes."

"Raja, stop Raja. Do you have any such pet names?"

"No. The photograph taken in the studio also showed my old face. There was no change at all."

"Did the shopkeeper recognize you?"

'He didn't notice at all. The girl was the only one who recognised me and smiled! She too left. I sat in the park and thought seriously about my plight. Somehow, I felt fully convinced that everybody had joined together to plot against me. I can do one thing. I will go home quietly when it becomes dark and eavesdrop on what they are talking."

"How can anybody go back to the same house?"

"Where else can I go? That's my house. My whole life revolves around it."

At night I go to the back side, jump over the wall of my own house, walk across the terrace and peep through the bedroom window.

On my bed, my wife is lying, the clothes on her body being removed one after another…

She says, "Put out the light!"

The light is switched off.

Oh my God! In my rage, I picked up the rope meant to hang the clothes on the terrace. A strong rope. Sufficient to kill them both.

I twisted the rope around my wrists so that it could be used easily. I will kill that rascal first, then Bhuvana. I banged against the door next to the window savagely with my shoulder as it was latched from inside. The latch broke and I almost fell inside.

I managed to stand. Bhuvana gathered her sari around her. She screeched in fear and ran to a corner. I moved closer to him. "How dare you come into my house and spend amorous time with my wife? You slut! Don't you have any shame? Are you a dog? Are you not born in a good family? Won't your father fret and fume when he hears about this? If Shobha happens to see the two of you in such a compromising position, won't she feel deeply hurt?

Is it fair for you both to do this? I will finish both of you today. "

I jumped on him and dropped the rope around his neck. By mistake it fell on his shoulder. I tightened it.

"*Aiyyo*! *Aiyyo*! Police! Police! Bhuvana, run and get somebody."

"Somebody please come! Any one of you please, hurry and come."

"If you are brave, let's fight one against one."

Bhuvana runs away. My noose falls in place. I strangle his neck… but before I can kill him about ten to fifteen people jump on me. They catch me and kick me. Everybody joins in and thrashes me. My whole body has bruises.

They arrested me in the night and kept me in police custody. Our company calender is hanging in the police station. The Inspector is known to me. He pretends that he does not know me and locks me up. Both that rascal and the inspector write a detailed report about me. One writes and the other makes the complaint.

I rambled, shouted and screamed. The inspector jumped up, reached me in one stride and struck my under belly with his baton. I felt like crying again. It was very painful.

They all left. The head constable gave me water. I felt hungry. We both had something to eat with the remaining ten rupees.

"Why did you get into trouble? You appear to be a decent man. Why did you enter another man's house by breaking the door and with the woman…"

"Head constable sir, that is my house, my door, my wife!

Won't I get anyone to believe me?" I screamed and wondered

whether I would ever get someone who would believe me!

The next afternoon they produced me in the Presidency Magistrate's court for the preliminary hearing. The prosecuting inspector, a young boy, framed the charges against me. An old lawyer was appointed for my defence.

"Name?"

"Jawahar Vittal."

The Magistrate turned over the papers and asked, "Who is Jawahar Vittal among them?"

"Sir, it is the petitioner's name."

"Then who is the defendant?"

"He too calls himself Jawahar Vittal. Refuses to give his true name."

"Hello! What is your true name? Don't feel scared."

"Jawahar Vittal."

"Oh God! What sort of a case is this? Okay. That is Jawahar Vittal no1 and you are no 2. Is it okay by you?"

"No Sir, I am no 1."

"Is this a laughing matter? Speak up. Why did you do that?"

"Your Honour, the case should be slapped against him and not me. First you question him. He has taken over not only my house but usurped all my property, my name…has taken possession of my wife…"

"What is this?"

"We are going to question the lady also. She is also a witness in this case."

"Your Honour, everybody is plotting against me."

"Why should they plot against you?"

"I am not able to answer this...But everybody has conspired together...

"Pazhanivelu, is this the case?"

"This is not the case, your Honour. He entered into Jawahar Vittal's house and tried to strangle and kill him with a rope. We have slapped section 511 and 312 against him."

"What do you say no1?"

" Absolute slander, defamation!"

"But what is the proof that you are Jawahar Vittal?"

"Beg your pardon, your Honour! What is your name?"

"Govindarajulu."

"What is the proof that you are Govindarajulu? Your Honour! Can you imagine a person who is denied his identity, his near and dear ones and his familiar surroundings. If you can, then, I am in that position. Your Honour! Please listen to me. Fair judgement is expected in a court of law and protection for an innocent man like me...to establish the truth. If I am punished, all these would be destroyed."

"The people who are with me will identify me. I have a wife, son, an identity card and a passport. What is this Pazhanivelu?"

"This man is slightly off his mental balance. He talks in a peculiar manner."

The Magistrate's face hardened. "In that case, it comes under section 84. You cannot file a case against him."

"Sorry. He is not mad but pretends to be mad."

"Whatever it is, don't you know the law? That's my ruling.......Get him examined in a government mental hospital and procure a certificate. Let them write that this man is not mad. We can proceed with the case after getting the report from the Superintendent, Mental Hospital, Kilpauk. Is that clear?"

The inspector who accompanied me cursed and said, "You are a very troublesome person."

In the afternoon they brought me back to the prison. I remained there for the next two days in uncertainty. I was in a big hall with forty undertrial convicts. I struggled to sleep on the floor. I was reminded of Shobha. Bhuvana's face floated in my memory. Sometimes I had my own doubts. Were they right? Am I not Jawahar Vittal? If I am not Vittal, then who am I? To which city do I belong? What is my name?

No, no. I am definitely Vittal! The moment I enter the house I can smell the jasmine creepers, the champa's sweet scent, the smell of the new shoes in the entrance. The incense aroma in the living room, Shobha's peculiar baby smell, the pleasant smell of Selvi's Charlie perfume, cow's urine stink in the back yard. Then the jack fruit smell, then the smell of the girl!

"Is it 'Stop Raja' again?"

"Yes sir! Her image irritates me frequently. I can neither forget the face nor the smile. She is in a reclining position and calls me 'Raja.' Who is she? Her figure constantly troubles me."

"I was in prison for two days. The third day I travelled

in an ambulance. In the hospital the junior doctors asked me innumerable questions and noted down the answers on sheets of paper. They lifted me bodily, stuffed something in my mouth and gave shock treatment. They gave me injections. I have been brought to you after undergoing a lot of torture. You have listened to my whole story. They say that you are an eminent and reputed doctor. It seems that you are held in high esteem in Vienna and other places. What has happened to me? Doctor, please tell me what has happened to me?....Find out what is wrong with me.....please!"

Click!

The tape recorder stopped. Dr Vijaykumar straightened up. He said, "What do you say?"

Ganesh looked at Vasanth and asked, "What do you say?"

"It is a strange case, boss."

"Is that all? DrVijaykumar, did you test this man?"

"Yes. He is perfectly normal! He is definitely not mad."

Ganesh took out a cigarette and started thinking without lighting it. Vijaykumar continued, "Reflexes are normal. IQ is above average. There doesn't seem to be any discord in his mental faculties at all. We have conducted all the tests."

"Jawahar Vittal" said Ganesh. Vasanth lighted the cigarette.

"Is he pretending to be mad?"

"It is very difficult to say. He doesn't even pretend! He keeps repeating one thing alone. You also heard it. 'I am Jawahar Vittal, I am Jawahar Vittal.' That's all. The same music, the same refrain."

"Boss, I feel the clue lies in 'Stop Raja'!"

"He has mentioned about a girl he has seen in one or two places, but he doesn't know her identity. It could be a hallucination in his confused state of mind."

"Re-incarnation?"

"No. I don't believe in reincarnation theory. I can say just one thing alone. Whatever you have heard in the tape, he spoke in front of me. There was not even a slight trace of falsehood that could be seen in his eyes. A very strong obsession only could be felt. He firmly believes that he is Jawahar Vittal. He points out a number of things so that we believe him. He gives very minute details. He points out some of his wife's personal birth marks also. He says that she has a mole on her thigh."

Ganesh said, "Is that so?"

Vasanth said, "Has she really a mole there?"

"Who knows? But he may say this in the court also."

Ganesh looked around. Books and books alone! *The American Journal Of Psychiatry, Delusion And Dreams.*

Vasanth reversed the tape very fast. The view meter danced and made "kala bula" sounds. It was stopped at a place. "This is definitely not a case of reincarnation or any such thing. A case of impersonation? No. But Something much more serious than that…"

"It is a sort of a lane. A faint trace of jack fruit smell and very slight urine stink can be felt. The city seemed to be connected with some temple. No idea why I feel that way."

"A girl about twenty years old?"

"A girl about twenty !"

Vasanth marked this place with a small piece of paper and wound the tape.

Ganesh said, "It is better if we can identify that girl.....Doctor, what certificate did you give him?"

"The man is absolutely normal. The Magistrate Court has made just one enquiry. How is the mental health of this man? Whether he can distinguish between right and wrong, and good and bad. I have mentioned that he can."

"Where is he now?"

"In prison. The case is to be tried. Ganesh, just one thing alone bothers me. I am highly qualified. I have gone abroad and accumulated all the alphabets after my name. I wonder whether this man's psyche is beyond my intelligence and ability. Is he really a psychic case? Has he to be given any psychic treatment? What sort of a disease is this? Is this amnesia? No. Schizophrenia? No, definitely not. I have taken an ECG. Why, I have tried even giving him some Sodium Amytal!"

"Why doctor?"

"It will make you speak the truth. I use it occasionally! Again and again, 'I am Jawahar Vittal'!"

"So?"

"That is why I called you Ganesh. I know that you are very busy. Please do me a small favour."

"What?"

"Please meet him in the prison!"

"And after meeting him?"

"You meet him and talk to him! You just tell me your impression about him! His case is to be tried in the court. If you feel that he is speaking the truth after talking to him, then you may take his case. Though I have certified him normal, now I too get doubts. I wonder whether I have made a mistake? Is there anything beyond my knowledge and intelligence? If he is not Jawahar Vittal, then who is he?"

"He is asking that question himself boss."

"Ok. Doctor, first I will go and meet him."

"That's my request."

"Can we have the tape?"

"Definitely, why not?"

"We will return it later."

Dr Vijaykumar saw Ganesh and Vasanth till the entrance. About seven or eight people were waiting in the reception area. Everybody looked wealthy. What Vijaykumar earned as honorarium in the Government Mental Hospital in a month, he could recover from these people in a single day.

Eight cars were waiting outside. Ganesh looked for his Fiat. "Call me later. I am very much interested in this case…"

Ganesh started the car in the second gear and drove with one hand. The other hand held a lighted cigarette. At the traffic intersection near Dasaprakash, he said, "Vasanth, what do you think?"

"Boss, the clue lies in 'Stop Raja'."

"No, not that Vasanth. Suppose everybody close to you ganged up together and vehemently denied that you are not Vasanth, how would you prove your identity as Vasanth?"

"I don't think a young child would tell a lie boss. Whatever may be the motives of the others, I don't think it is possible to make a child tell lies!"

"Child, and a dog?"

"Yes, dog. What do you say to that? I feel that the man is cooking up some stories!"

"Then, in that case, why should Dr Vijaykumar call us and ask us to take the case with so much interest?"

"Let's go and meet the man, boss. Then...."

"Then?"

"That's all. It is just an open and shut case. He may not be insane at all. He may have some other ideas. Let's go and meet him to honour Dr Vijaykumar's request."

"How does he know about the birthmark on the thigh?"

"How is it possible? But does a mole really exist? Can I go and find out?"

"Shut up."

"Boss, why do you turn towards Egmore? Are we not going to the prison?"

"Before that we have to meet Rajendran!"

"Why?"

"We have to know the police version of the case."

ACP Rajendran said, "Welcome. How is it you have come here?"

Ganesh said, "Oh, nothing, specific, just like that."

"I know that you won't come without any reason. Tell me the case that you are interested in. Murugesan, get two coffees."

Ganesh sat down. Rajendran had a paper weight with London Tower on his table. "Had you been to Scotland Yard for training through Interpol."

"Yes."

"You went without informing anybody to avoid being pestered for getting gift items!"

"No, no! I had to go at short notice. I did call you and was told that you had gone to Bangalore. Tell me what you want! My colleague Anata Narayanan has gone there. Tell me what you want and I will ask him to get it."

Vasanth said, "What will we ask for? Two *Playboys* and two *Penthouses.*"

"Ananta Narayanan won't bring any of those things."

"Rajendran, a strange case concerning Jawahar Vittal. Preliminary Hearing is over recently and the man is in prison. His case is due for hearing."

"Tell me the case. I might have seen it."

"He has attacked a man accusing him of seizing his wife, daughter and property. The case is booked under Section 511."

"The Magistrate has referred the case to the mental hospital for a certificate..... Is it that case?"

"Yes."

"Our Manikavaskam is dealing with that. Are you taking up the case?"

Vasanth said, "Yes."

Ganesh said, "Not yet decided." Rajendran said at the same time, "I don't know the full details. How is he known to you?"

"Dr Vijaykumar, an honorary doctor in the Mental hospital is known to us. He has examined this man and certified that his mental equilibrium is stable. But he has a nagging doubt and played the tape for us which had recorded in detail all that the man said."

"Have you decided that he is insane? Are you going to plead under insanity section?"

"We have not yet seen the man! Before meeting him, we would like to know how strong is the police case?" Ganesh said with a smile.

"Ganesh, do you think we will take a case if it is not strong? Call Manikavaskam."

Ganesh checked himself and said, "Please don't misunderstand me. I may fight against you in this case. I am not asking you for the police's secret findings. I just want to know from which angle the police is going to fight this case! That's all."

"If Ganesh is the defence lawyer, then don't we have to be better prepared? It's good for us also. Have you seen Priya lately? How is your health? You have lost some weight."

Vasanth said, "He smokes a lot sir!"

"What about you? You spend four rupees on a *beeda* just to have *Baba 600* added to it. Rajendran, you raid all these *zarda beeda* shops. These must be destroyed. Many people sell opium..."

Rajendran introduced Manikavasakam who entered at that juncture. He appeared young. The eyes were sharp and alive with enthusiasm and curiosity. The handshake proved that his hands were strong. The uniform was well starched, flashy and belonged to the special category.

"Mr Manikavaskam, Ganesh, your opponent."

"Is it the Jawahar Vittal case? Welcome," he said with a smile.

Ganesh said, "Will the plea of insanity stand?"

"No, definitely not! The doctor's certificate is very strong. There is nothing wrong with the man. He is normal."

"Then, do all the identities pointed out by him tally?"

Manikavasakam said, "No," and cast a glance at Rajendran.

"He says that a photo of the lady and him is hanging upstairs."

"Mr Ganesh, if you want to plead from that angle, forget it immediately. We have checked thoroughly. Finger prints, SSLC certificate, photo, everything. There is no basis for your client to say that he is Jawahar Vittal."

"He has not yet become our client! We have not yet met the man."

Manikavasakam smiled and said with relish, "If that is so, don't take it up. Hopeless case. Will anybody believe this, anywhere? Wife, a small child, and that too, a girl; why, even their dog is conspiring against him. He argues that they don't recognise him! He repeats this refrain again and again but will this stand in any Court of Law?"

"Are you going to call the wife and child as witness?"

"Why do you think he is telling such a lie?"

"Who knows? May be he is slightly insane?"

"If insane, then the track of the case changes."

"Vasakam, don't use the term insanity at all! We have already got the certificate from the hospital."

"Has he any ulterior motive?"

"Rajendran, he has mentioned the books, the number of steps leading to the first floor, the name of the books on the shelf and how they are arranged!"

"But how?"

Ganesh got up and said, "Can I take leave of you?"

Vasanth said, " Boss, let's wait for the coffee which he has ordered."

As they were having coffee, Rajendran asked, "Do you propose to take the case?"

"First, I'll have to meet the man."

"What did you say? *Zarda beeda*?"

Manikavasakam intervened and said, "Sir, a man from UP was selling *beeda* with opium in Mylapore. We have already arrested and imprisoned him."

Ganesh took leave saying, "Ok, I'll make a move. All the best."

In the car he said, "What are you thinking?"

"No chance at all. I feel it is pointless to meet him."

"I would like to meet him definitely. What is the time now?

Are there any visiting hours for the prison?"

'We can try to enter by taking Rajendran's name."

Ganesh had not visited prisons that frequently. He had been to meet Kartar Singh in Tihar Jail when he was in Delhi. He had a vague recollection that he had been to Madras Central Jail once. Everything was new. The Superintendent was not familiar.

"Don't you know that there are specific hours to meet the inmates?"

Vasanth said, "Yes, we know, Sir."

"Then why have you chosen an untimely hour?"

Vasanth looked at the superintendent's name plate on the table. C Raghavachari was written on it. "Sir, Rajendran said, 'if you meet Raghavachari, he will oblige you. He is a good person'."

"Rajendran? DC?"

"Yes."

"Why didn't you tell me this earlier? Hey Chidambaram, take them! Chidambaram is a lifer….He murdered his wife. See how docile he is now, like a cow tethered to a pole. We have allotted him guard duty for his good behavior."

Chidambaram gave a shy smile.

Vasanth looked at him with some suspicion and said, "You walk slightly away from us."

Raghavachari said "You have not mentioned whom you want to meet."

"Jawahar Vittal, an undertrial."

"Can you see the hall in front of us? He is lodged there."

The hall had about 40 small cement platforms similar in appearance to those you find in a graveyard. The prisoners were either sitting, lying down, sleeping, or twisting and turning around in various poses. The prisoners' interest was kindled when Ganesh and Vasanth neared them. Chidambaram said, "Who is Jawahar Vittal?"

One man got up slowly. "Somebody has come to meet you."

When he came near the bars, Ganesh said, "Chidambaram, can you let him out? He won't run away. I stand guarantee for him."

"Chidambaram, what happened to the soap that I asked for?"

"Chidambaram, I have diarrhea for the last two days. Inform the Superintendent."Chidambaram didn't pay any attention to the pleas of "Chidambaram, Chidambaram……." He deftly opened the door and let out Jawahar Vittal alone.

Ganesh said, "Hello! Let's go to the shade of that tree."

The man who came out said, "Who are you?"

"I am Ganesh, a lawyer. This is Vasanth, my assistant."

"Ganesh! Oh Ganesh! Are you going to plead for me? Everybody is conspiring against me. They throw me around like a ball. My wife, daughter, my relatives, my neighbours and everybody has joined together to conspire against me. Ganesh, please save me at any cost." Ganesh appraised him as he lifted the edge of his shirt and wiped away his tears.

He was five and a half feet tall. One or two grey hairs could be seen in the fifteen day old stubble on his face. He had thick eyebrows. Had the moustache been trimmed it would look smart. The eyes revealed excessive sadness. There was not even an iota of falsehood in the eyes. He was crying piteously and the tears flowed down copiously and drenched his shirt.

"First, you stop crying, Vittal."

"Thank God! Do you at least believe that I am Jawahar Vittal?"

"No, not yet. But we have listened to all that you said to Dr Vijaykumar."

"How?"

"From the recording of the tape."

"Did he record everything?"

A flash of surprise could be detected in his moist eyes.

"Forget that. We will call you Jawahar Vittal."

"Yes, I am Jawahar Vittal."

"We are comrades. You don't have to tell any lies to us at all."

"Why would I tell any lies?"

"Are you Jawahar Vittal?"

"Yes."

"Your wife...."

"That rascal has usurped my wife. When I saw them both lying on the bed together, my whole body raged with fire...I became very angry..."

"We have listened to all those things. You are Jawahar Vittal. Do you know what case is slapped against you?"

"Yes, of course! Section 511, attempt to commit a crime!"

"Not only that; they have added impersonation also under 420. The reply you propose to give will not be accepted in any court of law. If, as you say, your wife, daughter and others are conspiring against you, how can it be proved?"

He wiped his eyes. "You can enquire at GKVel's! Our wedding photo—of her and me taken together. They would have the negative."

"What is the date?"

"May 25th, 1967."

"The police say that they have seen all the photographs. They say that it is not you!"

"Ganesh, even the police is not speaking the truth."

"Why, Mr Vittal? Why?"

He wrung his hands in exasperation and said, "I don't know."

Vasanth said, "Just a question or two about that girl."

The three were standing under the shade of the tree. As soon as Vasanth mentioned the girl, Jawahar Vittal's eyes became bright and he started breathing heavily.

" Mr Chandar, what can I say about her?"

"I am Vasanth."

"Sorry Mr Vasanth. What do I say about that girl…?"

"If you don't want to say anything, that's fine by us."

"It is not like that. I don't know what to say about her—who is she, what is her name, whether she is real or an illusion—I just have no idea at all. I am unable to say anything."

"Is that so? Is she another case just like you?"

He said with a trace of anger, "What do you mean by a 'case'?"

"Some illusion which is difficult to describe?"

Ganesh said, "Just a moment, Vasanth. Mister, you have mentioned that girl very frequently. What is it Vasanth?"

"About twenty years old. With a big red dot on her forehead, danglers in her ears, lot of flowers in her hair, chain with mango design and a single strand chain...."

"What a remarkable memory you have, especially if it is about a woman."

"Boss, I am retaining this information thinking that it may be useful to the case. If it is not required, I can easily erase it from my memory."

"You describe a girl in such great detail but deny that you know her."

"A golden key in the single strand chain."

"Enough, Vasanth."

Vittal narrowed his eyes and focused them over a distance. It was obvious that he was trying his level best to recollect her name or address or any other details.

Misty-eyed, he said, "Mr Ganesh, who is she?"

Ganesh looked at Vasanth and said, "Who?"

Vittal continued, "If only she can be identified.... I think she may hold the key to all my recent strange behaviour."

"How?"

"Because she is the only one who recognized me and gave me a friendly smile."

Vasanth, "A smile alone is not enough. She has not given her address. You said you saw her earlier in front of a theatre. Can you tell us where it is located? Or else is that also just plain fantasy? "

"No Sir, Pondy Bazaar…At that time I saw her in Pondy Bazaar…."

"Yes. You saw her in Pondy Bazaar. Then?"

"She just smiled at me, got into a parked car and drove away."

"Only that much of an identity?"

"Yes."

"Don't worry, Vasanth will find out."

"Is that so Mr Vasanth? If only you could produce that girl in front of me….."

"No! he may say that, but how is it possible? The girl whom he met in Pondy Bazaar. She had danglers, smiled at him and said 'Stop Raja.' If you say locate and bring her, is it possible? Have a heart, boss."

"Why do we need a Vasanth, if name, address, the specific identification marks of the house and the street where it is located are given?"

"There is definitely no chance at all. I am out of the game."

"Mister….what did you say your name was….? Vittal?"

"Look at that! Look at that! My own lawyer doesn't believe that I am Vittal." Once again tears welled up in his eyes.

"No! No! You are definitely Vittal! I do believe you. Don't shed tears. There are so many other things in the world which deserve tears."

"Mr Ganesh, I cry not only for my name, I am weeping in the prison since a fortnight for all that I have lost along with my name. How is it possible for me not to be Vittal? My grandfather's photo is on the wall in the front room. Just behind the photograph a small piece of plaster has peeled off. A small sticker is stuck in a corner in that place. You can go and verify that! How am I to know that if I am not Jawahar Vittal?"

"Yes, yes, ofcourse! You have pointed out a lot of details about that house."

"Not only my house, but I even know all the birth marks on my wife's body. My darling daughter Shobha has a mole as wide as a centimeter just above her navel. A white patch on her back."

"Can you point out any identification mark for Selvi?"

"For whom?"

"Shut up, Vasanth! Mr Vittal! You can point out all these identification marks when the case comes up for hearing. But before that, let's find out why they are all conspiring against you and fail to recognize you. A small matter, just before that. Your bail is to be arranged. Is there anybody who will stand surety for you?"

"The whole area can stand surety for me, Mr Ganesh! But as things stand, I don't think anybody will recognize my presence. The conspiracy runs that deep. My friends, relatives, police...."

"Why, even the dog in your house!"

"It barks at me, the devil! How much mutton have I fed him?"

"Boss, first we have to plan about the bail application."

"That depends on the police case. Till now only committal

trial has taken place. Ok, Mr Jawahar Vittal, we will meet you again. First we will try to get you released on bail. Don't worry. Be brave!"

Vittal wept holding Ganesh's hands. He touched them to his eyes with reverence as if in obeisance. "Since fifteen days, since fifteen days..." he began but unable to speak further, his unspoken words melted with tears.

Where was the pretension in that?

They thanked the Superintendent, reversed the car, changed the gear, then moved forward, crossed the bridge, turned to the right, crossed Central.....

"We have to drop this case. You can't make head or tail of it!'

"What?"

"We have to drop this case. It makes ones head spin."

"Vasanth! Vasanth, do you think he is telling lies?"

"It is very confusing. If both the parties speak the truth, no case can stand." Vasanth's golden words for that day!

"What is today's date."

"Stop Raja", Vasanth said these words softly to himself.

"Stop Raja!" again.

"Say something more, Raja!"

"Pinch me Raja....... Push this away by yourself, Raja....."

Ganesh said, "Stop Raja! You are exceeding the limits Raja!"

"Poetry, Boss, pure poetry."

"Let's enumerate. What is the police case?"

"That's well known! This man either broke a window or door,

entered into the house, tried to kill a couple when they were lying down together…"

"When the husband and wife were lying down together…..?"

"If they are not husband and wife, it provides an emotional reason for his actions."

Ganesh remained silent.

"Boss, why are you quiet?"

"No Vasanth, this case is not that easy. What he says is also true. They were definitely husband and wife. Something which connects both the statements, something…"

"How is it possible, Boss? If what he says is true, then those two……Oh! I follow what you are thinking." Vasanth whistled.

"Is it possible to find out who that girl is with the little information that we have?"

"We have to get the tape from Dr Vijayakumar and listen to it again."

"That's no problem at all. We ourselves can stand surety."

Ganesh said, "Yes."

The third day….

"Ok, ok! What does the evidence say? No need to read the whole thing."

"The police have done a thorough investigation. They have compared both the people's signatures with that of the original documents of Jawahar Vittal…..They have witnesses to prove that our client's signature is forged. So also, Bhuvana and the baby are also ready to be witnesses. That man has a sister-in-law, Selvi. I went and asked her the time. That girl is just playing the fool. Just teasing and making a fool of others."

"Did you collect the material?"

"Oh! Yea, Boss!"

"Then, that girl..?"

Vasanth pouted.

"Till now I have not found her. I have realized how difficult it is to locate a girl with a golden chain around her neck either getting in or getting out of a Herald in Pondy Bazaar. After trying for three days, I have realized that no other work can be more futile than this. Instead I can cut halaal meat."

'That's why you have returned after eating a *zarda beeda*."

"You always focus on my *beeda*. I have given up the habit."

"Oh! Since when? "

"Since the last ten minutes."

Ganesh looked at Vasanth who was spreading out the papers without blinking. He had written SBL on the board.

Ganesh thought to himself, how did I find this young man in jeans, with dishevelled hair which is never combed, cigarette dangling from the lips but who worked like a maniac! 'Oh my God! How lucky am I?'

"Vasanth, have they published the advertisement?"

"Boss, it is published in this morning's edition of three Tamil newspapers in Tirunelveli. *Malai Murasu*, *Dinamani* (Madurai edition) and *Dinamalar*. It is there in all the three."

"Read, I would like to hear it."

Vasanth read the advertisement which had appeared in the Southern editions of Tamil Nadu's newspapers.

"Let this be known to all the members of my family and all those who have a right over me. After the 20th of June I have no connection with any of them-Raja." Post box No: etc. etc..."Is this what you asked for?"

"Perfect!"

"Boss, honestly, I don't understand a single word of this! Why this advertisement? For whom is this advertisement?"

"I'll tell you! But definitely only after I get a reply."

Vittal was granted bail on Dr Vijaykumar and another person's surety. Hence, he was released from the prison a week prior to the hearing in the court.

As soon as he came out, without wasting any time, Vasanth took him to Pondy Bazaar. They spent almost the whole day trying to locate the girl in the market place. No luck at all!

"Look carefully, Sir. Do you need glasses?"

"No, I don't need glasses, Mr Vasanth."

"Can you see the cow over there?"

"I can see that cow very clearly. I can recognize that girl anywhere, in any dress. She is the only one….."

"Who smiled at you in recognition! You have said this a million times! Can I ask you a small question?"

"Go ahead."

"Who are you Sir?"

"Oh God! No, not again! You are going back to the beginning."

"Ok, leave it. You are Jawahar Vittal. Is that right?"

"Yes…yes….yes…."

"What is the Herald's colour? "

"Chocolate brown."

"How many cars can be in Madras of that colour? We can find out easily. You have to speak in the court as we instruct you. We will take care of the rest."

"When is the case?"

"The twenty- fourth. Is this the girl?"

"No Sir. She was taller than this girl." Day turned into night, but the tall girl could not be found anywhere.

Vasanth was hungry when he returned to the office with Jawahar Vittal. Ganesh was deeply engrossed with the paper work of a case .He looked up and asked, "Any luck?"

"No, could not find the girl."

"Sit down, Mr Vittal."

"My goodness! How many papers !"

"Sir, where is he going to spend the night?"

"Dr Vijaykumar has made arrangements at Hotel Swarna."

"Hope it is not a shady place!"

"Shut up Vasanth. Open the drawer. I have got a few basic things needed for this gentleman."

The drawer contained all the necessary things needed for daily use like a dhoti, a razor blade, vest and soap, which were all purchased recently. They were all brand new.

"Ganesh, I don't know how to thank you…"

"Don't stand on formalities. Go to the room and take some rest."

"Yours is a new case for us. I will drop you at Hotel Swarna. The name sounds familiar."

"Who bears the expense for all this?"

"Why do you worry? Let things move as long as they can without any hitches."

"As soon as I regain my position, I'll return everything doublefold."

Vasanth said,"It is alright. You seem to be getting everything by the grace of others."

"But for how long, Mr Ganesh?"

"I have no idea. The three of us, Dr Vijaykumar, Vasanth and myself have you with us but we wonder what to do with you. We don't know who you are. First and foremost, you need an identity, a name and an address. You need a memory for names."

"Nothing is needed. I have no doubt about who I am. Don't worry on that count."

Ganesh looked at Vasanth with raised eyebrows and said, "Vasanth, can you drop this gentleman at the hotel?"

"No, Sir, I can go there on my own by an auto."

Ganesh whistled and said, "What a strange person," looking at the direction taken by Mr Vittal.

"Can't make out head or tail. How do we argue his case, Boss?"

" Can plead guilty. Having been afflicted by a bout of mental disorder, the confused thoughts lead me to believe somebody else's wife is mine...."

"Will be awarded two years."

"Is there any other option? Do you think he will confess like that? Even now the refrain has not changed—I am Jawahar Vittal."

Ganesh smiled and said, "Probably this is the first time in history, where the lawyer doesn't know his client's true identity and name..... What is it?"

"Boss, did you see this letter? It has come in today's mail."

"I haven't seen today's mail at all. Tell me what it is."

"A reply to our Tirunelveli advertisement."

"Read."

"Dear post box No: 9081. As regards your advertisement published in June 13th issue of *Dinamalar*, I am perplexed by it. My brother's name is Raja. He is missing since the last few days. Your name is also Raja. Which Raja ? What is your full name? Write immediately to the following address. Inform my brother's wife in Chennai. Her address is, Mrs Saroja, 128, ICF Colony, Perambur."

"What do you say to this? This is a Palayamkottai address."

Ganesh said, "Thank god!"

"What?"

"This is the very first break in this case."

"Boss, you said that you would tell me after getting a reply. I can't understand this at all. What is the significance of this advertisement? What does this reply mean?"

"Vasanth, did you notice anything special about

Vittal's speech?"

"Nothing specific. His dialect sounded like that of a person from Madras."

"The dialect is that of a person in Madras for a long time. But did you notice something very specific while talking? Do you remember the words that he used while describing the girl in Pondy Bazaar?"

"Yes....I do remember."

" The dialect that he used when he said, 'I saw her in Pondy Bazaar.' Does it remind you of any particular region of Tamil Nadu?"

Vasanth thought for a moment and said, "Tirunelveli district. Boss, brilliant."

"You are a tube light. If you get addicted to *zarda beeda*, this will be the result."

'That girl is the only one who recognized him. She called him Raja! Probably, his true name is Raja and he is from Tirunelveli....."

"Beautiful, Boss!"

'What do you propose to do tomorrow....?"

"I will enquire at the ICF address."

"Before that, Mr Reddy's case is looming large in front of us. Tomorrow is the hearing. I have not read a single line carefully."

In less than ten minutes, they both forgot all about Jawahar Vittal and were deeply engrossed in the peculiarities of another case. The smoke-rings of cigarettes hung in the air. The ordered food was delivered and waited for them. Outside the office, the sound from the retailers got subdued, cart-pullers went to sleep, the dark lanes got ready for their attractive sinful deeds, small children with gunny bags much bigger than themselves started collecting the city's garbage.

The shrill ringing of the telephone disturbed the silence.

"Ganesh," he said in a sleepy voice.

"Ganesh, Dr Vijaykumar."

"Oh! Hello Doctor! How come at this time?"

"Where did you leave that man?"

"Why? In Hotel Swarna."

"Did you drop him?"

"No. He said that he would hire an auto and go there."

"No, no. You should have dropped him there, Ganesh!"

"Why Doctor?"

"He did not reach the hotel at all."

"Is that so?"Ganesh looked at his wrist watch. It is almost five hours since he had left the place.

"Boss, what happened?"

"Doctor, you wait for another hour. Get back to me if he doesn't turn up! Did you go there to meet him?"

"No. I rang the hotel to find out whether he had reached. I wanted to conduct another couple of tests on him. Ganesh, I thought you would take good care of him, but you have been very careless."

"Doctor, but you have certified him as normal! Is it wrong to send a normal man all by himself to a hotel in an auto?"

"You are right, Mr Ganesh! But you have forgotten one thing. The man has come out on bail! I stand surety for him. At least on this count, surely you should have been more careful?"

"Sorry, Doctor! Let's wait till the morning. If he doesn't turn up, it is my responsibility to find him. Don't worry." Ganesh put the phone down and started thinking.

"Boss, has he not yet reached there?"

"No."

"I thought so. I had a vague doubt in my mind."

"Felt!....a vague doubt! You tell me now!"

"Where has this man disappeared? Big headache."

When they rang Hotel Swarna the next morning, they were told that Jawahar Vttal never came to the hotel.

"What a hopeless case! First the client said he had lost his name. Now the client himself has disappeared."

"We will get into trouble if we inform the police. We have to search for him in secrecy without anybody's knowledge. Oh God! Have we to look for one Jawahar Vittal in such a big city as Madras?"

The telephone rang.

"You answer the telephone. If it is Vijaykumar, tell him that I am not available."

Vasanth picked up the phone and said, "Central station enquiry."

"Sorry, wrong number." The telephone got disconnected.

It was Dr Vijay Kumar.

Vasanth left the telephone receiver off the hook and said, "Just tell me what you want me to do."

Ganesh gave a lop-sided smile and said, "I can't help smiling even in this crisis. As soon as the court session is over, let us go to the ICF address. I don't have much hope in that either."

In the evening they crossed the Perambur Railway Hospital.....the long road adjacent to the railway line and reached the government quarters. The quarters looked like cardboard boxes, all similar in appearance. It became dark before they could locate no128.

The house was fenced with rattan stems and had a small garden of a couple of square yards. It had a name plate at the gate which read M Rajasekaran, LME.

A young boy in shorts said, "Whom do you want to meet?"

'We want to meet Saroja."

The boy ran into the house shouting "Mamma..."

A girl who was even younger than him appeared and enquired, "Who?"

Vasanth said, "Mamma."

She ran inside screaming, "Mamma...., somebody has come to meet you." Not bothering about the slipping down briefs.

A woman, about thirty years old, came out. She had a bindi between her eyebrows. She was disentangling her hair with her fingers. Her eyes reflected some recent anxieties. Dark circles could be seen around them. The lips were soft. She looked at Ganesh suspiciously and asked, "Who are you?"

"I am Ganesh, a lawyer. We have come to find out a few things about Mr Raja."

"He came back only this morning and is sleeping."

"Oh! Has he come back?"

"How do you know him?"

"It is not that we know him..."

Ganesh looked at the man who appeared just behind her yawning with sleepy eyes and who said, "Who is that?"

"Hello, Mr Jawahar Vittal."

Even under the thin veil of twilight, there was no doubt at all. Definitely Jawahar Vittal! The facial features and the build of the body—all resembled him. But Ganesh felt that there was a subtle change in the mannerisms. The surprise and shock of meeting him at this house took a minute to subside. With a slight hunch and the fear wiped from his eyes, Jawahar Vittal looked like an excellent version of an expert actor .

He said, "Who are you?"

Vasanth said in a shocked tone, "Hey! Don't you know us?"

"If you say who you are, then it would be a great help." Why had the voice changed?

Ganesh and Vasanth looked at each other. "Mr Vittal, enough of this playing the fool. We have released you on bail, and you are hiding here! You can't do these sort of things!"

"What are you saying? Bail? Release ? Hiding? "

"Mr Vittal!"

"First and foremost, I am not Vittal.I am Raja."

"What?"

The wife said with fear in her voice, "What is it dear?"

"I don't know these two people at all. They have come here looking for somebody else."

"Who is it Dad?"

"What nonsense is this?" said Vasanth in a disgusted tone.

"Who are these people?"

"I told you, I don't know them," he snapped at his wife.

The frightened wife looked ten years younger than him. With small eyes, small breasts and with a short plait she resembled a traditional wooden doll.

The child came from inside and climbed on to her.

"Mr Vittal, do you want me to call the police?"

"Police? Why police? What have I done?"

"Why do you talk to them unnecessarily? You better come inside."

"They have slapped a murder case on you. You are released on bail. Your name is Jawahar Vittal."

"Dear, where have you been?"

"Keep quiet Kamalam, they are talking about somebody else. Sir, I am not Jawahar Vittal but Raja. I am a foreman in ICF.

"Are you from Tirunelveli?"

"Yes."

"Were you missing recently?"

He looked at his wife. She said, "Whether he was missing or

not, how does it matter to you? You just mind your own business and go away. Dear, you come inside." And she pulled him inside.

Ganesh said, "Look here, Madam, was your husband missing for a few days? Ask him what he did during that time."

"Dear, what did you do?"

"Kamalam, I don't remember anything at all."

The neighbours started collecting there one after another and they asked, "Raja, what is this commotion about?"

"He has returned home already in a distressed condition. These two people are harassing him."

"Who are you?'

"I am Ganesh and he is Vasanth."

A well-built man said, "Look here Mister! If you have anything to say, talk to me. Leave Raja alone. He has returned home just now."

"Ask him where he was in the intervening period?"

"Last week two well-dressed men were seen in our colony. They were roaming in front of Manjula madam's house waiting for a suitable opportunity to break in. Could it be these two men? What do you say Danapal?"

"Hey you! Mind your words."

"Vasanth, don't pick up a quarrel. Come, let's leave." So saying, Ganesh left the place abruptly. Two people came to thrash Vasanth but he dodged them by bending down. About ten to fifteen people collected there. They came running saying, "tie up both of them." Both Ganesh and Vasanth got into the parked

Fiat quickly. Before they could start the car and escape, wet mud was splashed against the rolled up window and it got stuck on the glass. The car raced ahead.

As soon as the danger became slightly mitigated, Vasanth rolled down one of the windows.

"Vasanth, is he the man?"

"Boss! Yes, he is the same man. He is just pretending. When we got into the car in a hurry, I turned and looked at him. His eyes revealed a puzzled and perplexed look. Once again he is telling lies."

"First, we have to inform Dr Vijaykumar. He stands surety for him. He should know where he is staying. Then we can inform Rajendran. If needed, let him be arrested. Are you sure that it is him?"

"There is no doubt at all, Boss. The very same man. There, Jawahar Vittal and here, Raja, ICF foreman. So what happened to Jawahar Vittal?"

"Has he discarded his identity and handed it over to someone else?"

"Don't confuse me."

"Would you like to have a *beeda*? It will make your mind vigourous."

"Oh God! Have you started keeping a stock in your pockets?"

Even though Ganesh was driving the car, his mind was deeply engrossed with the recent developments. The person who called himself Raja for a few days was none other than the Raja of 'Stop Raja.'

"Vasanth, did you manage to locate the girl?"

"No."

"Did you find out about the negative copy at GKVel's."

"Yes. They said that it was with the police."

Silence.

"Has Dr Vijaykumar lost five thousand rupees?"

"No. The man has not run away. He is very much in this city. If anybody asks for him, we can point to the ICF colony. Can they be twins?"

"I don't think so. Think again. How did we go to ICF colony?"

"On the basis of what he said repeatedly about the girl who said 'Stop Raja' and the Tirunelveli dialect spoken by him, we placed an advertisement in the Southern region papers….."

"So ICF Raja had disappeared for a few days, called himself Jawahar Vittal during that period and has now returned as Raja again. That's it, in a nutshell."

"But why did he do that?"

"Ask me another!"

"Have they all joined together and are taking us for a ride?"

"No. Is it a scheme to kill Jawahar Vittal?"

"Silly! Do you think a person intending to murder will make it public like this? No, Vasanth, it is something much deeper than that. Something sinister, though I am not able to say what it is. This is just the tip of the iceberg. We have to inform Rajendran immediately without wasting any time."

He called Assistant Commissioner Rajendran the moment he reached the office.

"Yes, Ganesh."

"Rajendran, do you remember Jawahar Vittal's case? We had got him released on bail. He just disappeared all of a sudden. We were shocked. By chance I came to know that he could be the missing person from ICF colony. We located him there when we went to make enquiries. But he calls himself by a different name."

"Is that so?"

"If you want to re-arrest him, I can give you the address."

"No need. We have dropped the case."

"What?"

"Jawahar Vittal, who had made the complaint, has withdrawn the case. He made a request to me also. If the case is heard in the court, then his wife and daughter would be called as witnesses. There they may have to reveal identification marks on their private parts and it may lead to embarrassment. Hence, he requested not to proceed with the case. So we have dropped the case. Though the doctor had certified the man as normal, did he not appear to be slightly insane? We have also dropped that. Inform the doctor. You also don't search for him anymore."

"Is that all?"

Vasanth asked, "What happened, Boss?" as soon as Ganesh put down the receiver. Ganesh thought for a moment and said, "The police is not proceeding with the case."

"Why?"

"The complainant has withdrawn the case."

"Thank god, the confusion is sorted out."

"Why Vasanth, why? Why did he do that?"

"He is insane, that's why."

"What did Vijaykumar say?"

"He is not insane. What does it matter? Come on, Boss, let's have a cup of coffee."

"Everybody joined together and drove us mad."

"What's happened now? Nothing. We have roamed around for a couple of days, that's all. Leave it. Let's look into Narayana Reddy's case. Boss, I have to go to Mambalam."

Ganesh stared ahead with unseeing eyes. "If only we had found that girl!"

"As Hegel says, you can't see black cows on a dark night. What we need just now is black coffee. Let's go."

The next evening, on their way to Thyagaraya Nagar in connection with a case, they met Dr Vijaykumar and informed him about the developments.

Vittal's escape, how he was found in Perambur where he was living with his family as Raja , and when questioned about what had happened earlier, staring without any comprehension....

"Did you notice his eyes when he said that?"

"Yes. He did not seem to be telling lies. He seemed to be slightly apprehensive and this could be detected in his eyes. Doctor, why did he come all the way from Perambur to Peter's road and create a ruckus there? How did he know so many private things about Jawahar Vittal? How did he manage to forget all these things so quickly?"

The doctor thought for a few seconds and said, "No idea. I am unable to answer this question."

"Just one assumption alone seems to fit. He is insane."

"As far as my investigation of him goes, he is definitely not insane."

"Anyway, the case is closed. A man came from somewhere, drove us mad and then returned back to Perambur as Raja, Foreman, Integral Coach Factory! Good night!"

After meeting the doctor, they went to Mambalam. It was almost half-past-six in the evening. It was overflowing with people coming out of theatres. Ganesh and Vasanth had coffee in Pondy Bazaar. Narayana Reddy had not yet returned from the studio. They strolled in the market to while away the time.

"Vasanth, do you know that there was a bookstall in Pondy Bazaar in the olden days?"

"I don't know. Probably I was not born at that time."

"*Tamil Pannai*. Now a hotel is occupying that space."

"The person who does not run a textile shop cannot survive here."

"Jewellery?"

"Jewellery shops can be run only by big giants."

Ganesh wanted to buy vests so he entered a supermarket. It was centrally air-conditioned and spread over a large area containing a ground level as well as a first floor.

"Size 38, without sleeves, interlock, Tantex. Give me two of these."

"Boss, see there."

"Where?"

"That side, where the saris are sold. Do you see the girl in the blue sari?"

"She is pretty."

"Look at her just below the neck."

"Hey!"

"Boss, look."

Ganesh looked at her. She was wearing a chain.

"Look at the pendant of her chain. A golden key. Do you remember?"

Ganesh tried to recollect the golden key in his mind.

"Oh yes! the 'Hey Raja stop' girl." Jawahar Vittal informed us that the girl had a golden key as a pendant in her chain."

The girl paid the bill and left the shop with the sari packet and got into a chocolate brown Herald.

The car started very quickly and mingled with the traffic in the street. It overtook a tempo and an auto, honked loudly for the Pallavan transport bus to give way and moved forward quickly. Ganesh dashed after it in his Fiat. He followed the direction taken by the Herald. Luckily they saw the Herald waiting for the signal at the traffic intersection at Teynampet crossing. Ganesh stopped his Fiat just behind the Herald. He could also see a man in the driver's seat. He could see the thick and luxuriant hair of the girl sitting next to him. The man was talking to her. When the light changed to amber, Ganesh honked and the man slightly turned his head and saw Ganesh. Thick moustache, rimless glasses.

Ganesh followed the car very closely. "Is she the girl, Vasanth?"

"Chocolate Herald, girl, key in chain. Three points tally Boss."

The car turned into Mount Road. It went over the flyover to Spencers and once again got caught by a red light. It turned to the left as soon as the light turned green and stopped at Connemara. They both got down and went into the library.

Ganesh and Vasanth got down from their car but without wasting time in locking it, they followed them into the library. Both the man and the girl were waiting in the lounge. The man seemed to be about forty years old. The moustache covered half his face. He wore a checked shirt. His mannerisms and his clothes gave the impression that he was foreign returned. The musk scent which emanated from him appeared imported.

The girl was in a silk sari. Her breasts seemed to be over sized. Vasanth wondered whether they were real or enhanced. He decided that this could be decided only by touch. The thin lips had a slight trace of red lipstick. She looked like a model in an advertisement pushing away her blow dried and shampooed hair.

They didn't speak much to each other. They were sitting on the cushioned seats and seemed to be waiting for somebody.

A little later, a six-and-a-half foot tall foreigner came into the library. The man went and shook hands with him while the girl stood a little away in respect and awe. She folded her hands in greeting. The foreigner, though very tall, was wearing shorts and flip flops. He appeared as strong as the central pillar in a temple. His height made him bend his head while talking to them. All three entered the *Kolam* restaurant.

Vasanth looked at Ganesh and said, "What to do, Boss?"

"I am hungry. We can have some snacks while watching them. Come, let's go in."

The AC was soothing. The light was dim. A pop-group was singing Boney M's *Silent Lover* tolerably well. They could not spot the three of them. They looked at each and every table thoroughly. There was a Parsi family, an old foreign couple, two young men and a Gujarati family occupying a full table.

What had happened to those three people? They were definitely not there.

Vasanth said, "This is surprising, Boss."

"Vasanth, they must have known for certain that we followed them here."

A man who was in charge of table reservation came near them and said, "Yes, Sir, may I help you?"

"What is your name?"

"Fredrick."

"Do you know Tamil?"

"I am from Royapuram, Sir."

"That's nice, Fredrick. Just now, a foreigner and our own people, a man and a woman...."

"Yes, Sir, they were here. They left just now."

"Did they go by the front entrance?"

"No, they left by the pantry entrance."

Ganesh said, "Is that so?" He looked at Vasanth with a sense of having been cheated. Fredrick said, "Are you police?"

They came outside in a hurry without wasting any time to answer his query. The Herald was not there. "They have cheated us very easily. They knew for certain that we were following them."

"Probably, we made a mistake by following them too closely."

"Probably. Did you notice the car number?"

"Yes— MSR 6622."

They drove to the RTO office

"Did you ask for MSR 6622?"

"Yes, Inspector."

"It is registered in the name of Dr Srinivasamurthy, Udaya Poly Clinic."

"Do you have the address?"

"Are you known to Rajendran?"

"We are almost related to him."

"Please, take a seat. Will you have some coffee?"

'No, we are in a bit of a hurry."

"You may come to the RTO office at any time. Tangaraju of OR section is known to everybody and any one will guide you to me."

"Thanks. That address?"

"43, CP Kovil street, Mylapore."

Crossing the tank and turning to the left they came to a lane.

It could not be called a street. After crossing the brass vessels shops, lingerie shops and very old, original, Mylapore lawyers' houses, they saw Udaya Poly Clinic in a new building which was constructed by demolishing two old houses. The chocolate coloured Herald was parked in front of the clinic, blocking the lane. As they passed through the lane, they were enveloped by a strong smell of jackfruit. They could also smell urine.

Vasanth said, "This is the place, Boss."

They entered the clinic. About ten to fifteen people were waiting. There were empty chairs too. It was obvious that the clinic was run by two or three doctors who were out to fleece people. Each and every doctor had a separate cabin with his name plate on the door. But the reception area was common to all. There was a round table with a white telephone which resembled a small white rabbit, a small desk calculator and a porcelain flower vase with fresh flowers. That girl was sitting on the receptionist's seat. The same girl! The golden key was dangling prominently from her golden chain.

"Boss, the girl is very pretty even at close quarters."

"Shut up."

They went near her. She looked at them with her big eyes and said, "Can you please tell the name of the doctor you want to consult?"

Ganesh said, "Not the doctor, but you."

She looked at them indecisively and called, "Shiva." She said, "Sorry, but I am on duty."

"When does your duty get over?"

"Why?"

"We want to meet you."

"Why?"

"To speak with you."

"What do you want to speak about?"

"About ICF Raja."

She looked surprised.

"ICF Raja? What does it mean?"

"ICF Raja is a man, a person. He said he knows you."

"I don't know any Raja."

Vasanth said, "Hey Raja, stop! Don't you remember."

By now Shiva, the watchman had came near her table.

"What is the problem, Madam?"

"Shiva, they are asking me about some unknown person and troubling me when I am busy. I don't know what they are asking and they are creating trouble."

"Hey! Who are you?"

The buzzer of the telephone sounded. The girl picked it up and said, "Yes Doctor, not at all Doctor." Her eyes expressed perplexity.

"Can you make a move? See, all the patients are looking at us." Shiva tried to push Ganesh away by keeping a hand on his chest. Ganesh brushed the hand away and said, "Miss, it is not good for you to tell lies. You will be in trouble later. I am Ganesh, a lawyer. There are too many Ganesh's in the telephone directory.

So I have given my name with two n's, Gann...."

"Just get lost, I say!"

"Don't worry, Boss. Give me two day's time. I will find out everything about that girl. How many moles on her body....Has she not a slight resemblance to Sripriya?"

"She is telling lies, Vasanth!"

"I don't think I can say that with so much certainty. But don't you see that what that man Jawahar Vittal alias Raja described in the tape fits that place. He said a place like a temple. Jack fruit smell....He had come down this lane."

"But he didn't say Mylapore. He said a city connected with a temple. Vasanth, there are too many questions in this case which don't have an answer. Take out a paper and a pencil. Write."

Vasanth looked for a pencil among the numerous books spread across Ganesh's table. Ganesh started dictating with both his eyes closed. As he dictated, both his index fingers were caressing the bridge of his nose in deep concentration.

Why did ICF Raja go to Peter's road, call himself Jawahar Vittal and create a ruckus?

Why was the case against him withdrawn so quickly?

Why did Raja go to Udaya Poly Clinic in Mylapore from Perambur?

It seemed like a collage of separate incidents. In this collage, who was speaking the truth and who was speaking lies?

Why do we still hold on to it with obstinancy when all the others have given up?

"If you want I can answer the last question, Boss."

"Yes, speak up."

"Nothing but sheer impudence." said Vasanth.

"No Vasanth, curiosity. Lawyer Ganesh has no work at all in this case. It has come out of the court. Raja has gone back to his house. The curtain is pulled down on the act. Even then, as far as this case is concerned, it tantalizes me. If a girl's hand and a small toe alone is seen, is not your interest kindled to see her fully?"

"Boss, we may lose our sanity before that. This case is not going to give us any monetary benefit. To begin with, we don't even know who our client is. Somebody comes in calling himself Vittal. A doctor requests us to take up the case. Before we can do that, the man disappears and becomes ICF Raja. He says, 'Oh my God, I have never set eyes on you in my life.' And this girl.... can't say without proof,....good merchandise.....looks like she may be playing the fool."

"Have you heard of the theatre of the absurd?"

"Boss, don't involve me in all these intellectual pursuits. I can answer only about Tina Munim."

Ganesh picked up the telephone as it started ringing.

"Mr Ganesh?"

"Speaking."

"I am Hemlata."

Ganesh immediately recognized the voice. "Udaya Poly Clinic receptionist?"

"Yes."

"Speak up."

"I would like to speak to you alone about your enquiry in the clinic. Can you come to my house?"

"Yes, of course," said Ganesh.

Both Ganesh and Vasanth went to the girl's house in the evening. She lived in a lane branching off from Royapettah High road. The houses in that lane were quiet because the noise of the main road did not reach there. The girl was living in the rear portion of one of these houses.

She was waiting restlessly for their arrival. The perspiration on the girl's face and neck when she opened the door was an indication of her inner turmoil.

"Thank God! You have come. I was about to ring you up again. Please take your seat. What will you have?" She was very young. She looked not a day more than nineteen. She could pass even as a sixteen-year-old. The golden key was dangling in the chain which had helped to identify her. Thin lips and shaped eyebrows. She looked like a girl who could write a book on how to wear minimum make up but at the same time look glamourous .

"I am Vasanth and this is Ganesh."

"You want to know my name, don't you?"

"Preeti," said Vasanth.

"Hey! How do you know that?"

"The moment I saw your face, I somehow felt that it had to be Preeti. Besides, your eyes were an indication."

Ganesh said, "We found out from your office."

"Why did you let the cat out of the bag, Boss?"

"Ganesh, how did you come there looking for me?"

"The golden key in your chain and the Herald."

"Ganesh, that's the doctor's car. Just a small request, don't mention the case to anybody."

"Which case?"

"Mr Raja's case."

"Why?"

"It is a very complicated and a confusing case. I myself do not know the full details."

"Are you advising us without knowing the full details?"

"I know for certain that this is a dangerous mission."

"What do you know?"

"All I know is that in this incident, I have played only a small role."

"Ok, tell us."

" What I am going to tell you…."

"Shhhh…..proceed."

"Where to begin and how to start? Why don't you do one thing? You ask me all the questions you came to ask. To the extent I know, I will answer truthfully."

Ganesh said, "Ok, Vasanth, fire!"

Vasanth cleared his throat. "For how long do you know Mr Raja?"

"About two months."

"How do you know him?"

"It was I who brought him to the clinic."

"Come again. Did you bring him?"

"Yes, of course!"

"Where did you go?"

"I went to Perambur."

"How did you know his address in Perambur?"

"It was given at the clinic."

"Who gave you the address?"

"Dr Balagopal and Dr Kenneth."

"Dr Kenneth? Who is he?"

"He is an American."

Vasanth looked at Ganesh who said, "Mmmm… go ahead!"

"So Dr Balagopal gave you Raja's Perambur address and asked you to bring him. But why? "

"They didn't give me any reason. They asked me to bring him somehow or the other."

"Somehow or the other?"

"Yes."

"How did you bring him?"

"I saw Raja coming out of the house and walking towards the bus stand. I too walked along with him. I asked him where the taxi stand was. I asked him for the time. He answered me and showed me. That day I left it at that. The next day I met him at the bus stand. I smiled at him. He reciprocated with a smile. I told him my name. He told me that his name was Raja. I told him that it was a good name. I called him on the phone one day. Another day, I called him to see a film with me."

"But why did you do all these things?"

"Balagopal promised to give me two thousand rupees if I brought him somehow or other."

Vasanth said,"What did you do with the two thousand rupees?"

Ganesh continued, "You brought him to the clinic. Then what happened?"

"Mr Ganesh, I don't know exactly what happened after that. But what I can say is that Dr Balagopal had almost imprisoned him. Once I saw Raja in one of the rooms. He was lying down and his EEG was being monitored. There was a small red spot just above his forehead. Dr Balagopal was taking two or three cc of blood. Then, once again, I saw him in the same room. He was sitting cross-legged. He was awake. I smiled at him. He got up and walked. I said, "Hey Raja, stop." He turned around and said clearly, "I am not Raja, but Vittal."

"Interesting," said Ganesh.

"After that I did not meet him for many days. Just once I saw him in a hurry after shopping with the doctor in Pondy Bazaar. I smiled at him. He looked pitiable and had the look of a lost person. I told the doctor about it. He told me harshly not to talk about him anymore. That's all I know."

"Miss Preeti, who is Dr Kenneth?"

"He is a good person. He is a visiting professor from the USA. He is supposed to be an expert in psychiatry. He is Dr Balagopal's classmate."

"Did he also ask you to bring Raja? Think clearly before answering."

"Yes. He also said that."

Ganesh was pensive for some time. "Yes, but why are you telling all these things to us?"

"I have a feeling that both the doctors have joined together and done an experiment on him. This might have led the man to incur some injury or memory loss in some way. My conscience is pricking me that I might have done something wrong. I have been used to lure Raja to this place. Two thousand rupees is a big amount for that. I have a feeling that something sinister is taking place without the knowledge of other staff members. Has anything happened to Raja?"

"Everything has happened."

"Has he gone? What a pity!"

"Not gone. He is very much alive. He called himself Vittal for a few days which led to some confusion…"

The door bell buzzed. "Somebody is at the door," said Ganesh. Preeti went towards the door and Ganesh looked around. An embroidered Gandhi was hanging on the wall. Beside it there were pictures of a duck, a lady with the likeness of Sarojini Naidu, Mantralaya Swami and Satya Saibaba. There was a JK Tyres calendar. Preeti's convocation photo was also there. Parvati Krishna Rao was written on a book on the table. Preeti's voice could be heard . "Hello Doctor! What a surprise?"

"I came this side to purchase cane chairs. I thought that I

would just drop in to say hello to your mother. Where is she?"

"She has gone out."

"May I come in?"

A slight hesitation. "Mmm…c….come inside, please."

He didn't seem to wait for her invitation at all. He came inside and looked at Ganesh and Vasanth. She said with some hesitation, "Doctor, they are Mr Ganesh and Vasanth…..they have come to meet ……me!"

"Did I not meet you both in the clinic yesterday?"

"Yes, you might have seen us there. Are you Dr Balagopal?"

"Yes."

"I am Ganesh, a lawyer. Mrs. Parvati Krishna Rao had called us. She has a litigation with regard to her uncle's land."

The suspicion in Dr Balagopal's deep observant eyes slightly lessened.

"Some judicial matter?"

"Yes Doctor," said Preeti.

Balagopal was about thirty-five years old. His dress was flashy. He had combed the few remaining scattered hair carefully and neatly, and his specs had a thick broad frame. His expression reflected that he had never experienced any interference in his life. Cunningness and intelligence could be discerned in his sharp eagle nose.

He said, "I have heard about you."

Vasanth said, "We have heard about you also."

He was jolted and said, "Who mentioned me?"

"Dr Vijaykumar."

"Oh! Good old Viji! Do you know him?"

"We know him very well."

"Anyway, Mr Ganesh, it is a pleasure to have met you." The doctor said with a smile, "See you later Preeti! Be careful with the court case. If you are caught in the clutches of a lawyer, it is very difficult to escape."

Ganesh said with the same equanimity, "Yes, definitely. Does this not apply to doctors also?"

As soon as he went away, Preeti said, "He has dropped in suspecting that I may contact you. I have lost my job."

"Why do you feel scared?"

"Because in the last two years, he has never ever visited my house. He has come just today."

"It might have happened just by chance!"

"No. Anyhow, Mr Ganesh, please leave."

"But you have not told us the whole thing."

"I have already told you everything."

"If we want to meet you again…?"

"Just give me a call. Can you please leave now?"

As soon as they came out of the house, Vasanth said,"What is this Boss? She invited us home but towards the end, she almost threw us out."

"Yes, the doctor's visit changed everything. She is scared of him. Did you understand anything of what she said?"

"No. Have to go home and think about it."

"I feel that tomorrow that girl will lose her job."

"Why?"

"Though Dr Balagopal pretended to be calm, did you notice that the tip of his nose was throbbing. He definitely did not approve of her meeting us or talking to us."

"Why?"

Ganesh started the car and drove very slowly. The traffic signal showed red at the intersection of Elliots Road and Royapettah High road.

"One Raja in ICF. He is brought to a Mylapore clinic by a girl. Then, a blank space. Then he calls himself Vittal…He goes to Vittal's house and causes disturbances. There he attempts to murder, but gets caught, goes to prison, comes out on bail and becomes ICF Raja again. What does it all mean?"

"Some thing evil. Green light, please start the car."

The car turned left to the beach side.

"Vasanth, a foreigner is also involved in this."

"Boss, it is difficult to follow your thoughts."

"Vasanth, is it possible to control a person's mind and memory with medicines?"

"Honestly, I don't know."

"I am giving you three days time. I want to get all the information on mind control experiments. Can you do this?"

"What are you saying? Are you implying that Raja's mind was changed with medicines to that of Vittal?"

Ganesh said, "It is something much more sinister than that."

Vasanth entered with a load of books held tightly. They covered his face. He placed them in front of Ganesh, took a deep breath saying, "Thank God."

"What is this?"

"All these books are on mind control."

"Did you buy them?"

"Me and buying! Everything is free. All from libraries—British Council, Connemara, United States. Boss, it is a very interesting field. Till 1930, they called a disease which occurred due to deficiency of B-complex as insanity… Do you know when tranquilizers were discovered? In 1950…Then there is a medicine, Thoracine… That single medicine emptied almost half the mental hospitals…"

As Vasanth was enumerating, Ganesh said, "Easy, easy…" and glanced at the books. *The Manipulation Of Human Behaviour, Brain Washing In Red China, TSD Report On Communist Control Technique.*

"Excellent! Did you read anything?"

"A lot, I have read a few pages here and there."

"What did you learn?"

"You can knead a person's mind as and how you like. You can manipulate him in different ways. There are medicines for everything. Hypnotism is used to manipulate the mind. Boss, everything is pure chemistry."

Ganesh picked up one of the books and glanced through it. He read, 'I can hypnotize a man without his knowledge or consent into committing treason.' "Who said this?"

"Dr George Eastabrookes, Chairman of the Department Of Psychology, Colgate University, Canada. Listen to this, Boss. In the World Wars, a few soldiers who were hit by bullets and whose hands were dangling loosely used to say, 'Mmm.., no pain at all.' How is this?"

"How?"

"It is due to Endorphin! The intoxicating drug which is secreted within our body."

"I don't follow. But it is obvious that you have read a lot. Vasanth, you have read a lot about mind control. Can you shed some light in connection with our client?"

"Boss, I can only make a guess."

"What is it?"

"Whatever I say is based on modern medicines and psychological control of the mind."

"For that only you have piled up a number of books! Go ahead..."

"But if you ask me the reason why this has happened, I'm sorry, I just have no answer."

"I won't ask you, speak up."

"That man's name is only Raja."

"Ok."

"Dr Balagopal studied psychiatry in the USA.

"Ok."

"He needed a person on whom he could experiment."

Vasanth, anticipating Ganesh's query said, "You can question me later. First let me finish what I have to say."

"Ok."

"Dr Balagopal needed a clinic. He needed a man to experiment on with medicines or a hypnotic method. He sends his receptionist with the specific instructions to bring ICF Raja, somehow or the other, to the clinic. He offers her good money as an incentive. If you ask me why he sent her all the way to ICF… when there could be suitable candidates in Mylapore itself, sorry, I have no answer. That girl goes to Perambur, meets and befriends Raja and brings him to this place, the clinic.....Here Dr Balagopal gives him some medicines which clash with his memories, make him forget all his original thoughts. He is forcibly fed all Jawahar's details within his mind. Don't laugh, Boss. If you had read these books, you would understand. Do you know what a Prefrontalsonic experiment is? Do you know what is Alpha rhythm? Do you know the consequences of cocaine consumption? And you are laughing at me!"

Ganesh, "Hey look! Don't bluff me with names that I have not read. I am not laughing. Tell me more."

"What I wanted to say was that all this is possible either with medication or with hypnotism."

"I believe you. Proceed."

" Raja escaped from the clinic while he was under treatment. He believed himself to be Jawahar Vittal, and as him created a ruckus. After that we know what happened—his release from prison on bail."

"After that?"

"As soon as he was released, Balagopal might have brought him to his clinic, given him an antidote and rekindled his original memory to that of Raja. Raja returns home. He does not remember what happened in between."

Ganesh tried his best not to laugh. " You want me to believe this?"

"You read these books, Boss. Stranger things than this have taken place! Do you know what is RHIC-EDOM?"

Ganesh did not answer.

"Radio Hypnotic Intra Cerebral Electronic Control And Dissolution Of Memory....Lincoln Lawrence, in 1967....."

"Vasanth, my head is spinning. I'll go through these books. Then I will tell you whether I believe your stories or not. Before that, let's take stock of the existing facts. ICF Raja has been used by Dr Balagopal for an experiment. Since he was used as a guinea pig, Raja called himself Jawahar Vittal and caused a lot of disturbance. We got him released on bail. Then suddenly he became normal. You filled up the blanks in some ways. After reading the books, I will tell you whether what you have filled up in the blanks is true or false. But there are too many holes in your story. What you do just now is to go and enquire of that girl some more details......" Ganesh thought for a second then said, "No, wait!"

"What is it, Boss?"

"No, no. If caught, I can't face Rajendran."

"Boss, I also thought about that."

"About what?"

"Breaking into Balagopal's clinic to make a thorough search for any clues."

"You rascal, how do you read my mind so accurately?"

"Is it not due to so many years of association with you? Boss, can we do that?"

"Breaking into the clinic?"

"You need not come."

"Are you going to do it alone?"

"No, I have a friend, Pakkirisami....in Robertsonpet. He has a knack with his fingers like a virgin..."

"Vasanth, no need for any comparisons."

"To open any lock."

""That clinic has a Godrej door lock."

"Hey Boss, you noticed that. Even at that time you had the intention to break into the clinic."

"I just looked at it."

"In that case, either tonight or tomorrow night we will get into the clinic by breaking the lock."

"If you are caught, don't tell your name at all."

"If they ask my name I will tell them that I am Subramania Bharathi."

"Hey! He was a great poet. If only you knew something about poetry...."

Vasanth interrupted and sang,

"Oh beautiful moon,
Your beauty seems enhanced
Although hiding behind
A thin veil of clouds."

He said, "Ok, Boss, I will call you at 8.30." He waved and left.

Ganesh was speechless.

He rang up Dr Balgopal's clinic. Preeti answered.

"Hello, I am Ganesh speaking."

"Yes, Mr Ganesh, what can I do for you?"

"Ganesh, the lawyer."

"Do you want to see Dr Balagopal?"

"I want to speak to you. When can I meet you?"

"Sorry, I don't know you." The telephone was disconnected.

Ganesh stared at the telephone for some time. Was she scared that Balagopal may eavesdrop? Or else, was she also a subject of his experiments...just like Raja?

He lit a cigarette. He used to smoke Wills, but after the budget, he downgraded the cigarette to Wills Flake. He was definitely going to stop this habit one of these days. The pleasant shock which he experienced hearing Vasanth reciting Bharati all of a sudden still lingered in his memory. Though his association with Vasanth was a fairly long one, spanning a few years, he yet had to understand him fully.

The telephone rang. He picked it up and said, "Hello!" carelessly.

"Mr Ganesh?"

"Yes, speaking."

"I am giving you twenty-four hours. If you don't stop all your monkey businesses within that specified time, you will meet a tragic end in a bloody road accident. You will be torn to pieces. There won't be a body to be cremated."

"Hello!"

The telephone was disconnected. Ganesh was thoughtful. Roaring male voice. Two words spoken in Tamil, 'Atharkull' as 'Atharkul' and 'Kazhanru' as 'Kajandru', had slightly different pronunciation, seemed as if somebody who did not know Tamil was reading from a piece of paper—Tamil words written in English.

Twenty four hours! The case was becoming fascinating. Suppose the threat was genuine and capable of actually being carried out?

Ganesh's last case! Vasanth called at 8.30 sharp. "I have met Pakkiri, Boss. After watching a film in Kamadhenu, we are both now going to the clinic."

"Vasanth, I have just received a threatening call from a stranger!"

"What about?"

"If I don't stop within twenty four hours, I will meet a gory death in a road accident."

"So, are you scared?"

"No, not yet."

"You should have said, 'you mother fucker, put the phone down'."

"Even if I had said that he would not have understood it.

The voice which spoke does not understand Tamil. Seemed to be reading what was written in English."

"So you have detected that much. You are a genius, Boss. Don't worry. Don't we have twenty four hours? We can easily lift up the whole Kapali temple within that period. That too, if our Pakkiri consumes a *Kamala*, that will do the trick. Good night!"

Ganesh became engrossed in the books.

He read the books through the night. He was not aware of the silence that descended upon the city—neither the loud criticism and review of the people after seeing the late show of films, nor the *thadak thadak*, noise of the first electric trains leaving the Beach station. None of these caught his attention. He postponed his sleep by saying 'just a little more' to his burning eyes which pleaded for some sleep. When he looked through the window, he was surprised to see the faint light of dawn. He stopped reading. Oh God! Is this possible?

Ganesh had underlined many places with his pencil in the books. He made many notes of his own.

'When you wake up from the hypnotic trance, you will be unaware of the messages imbedded deep within your mind.'

The notes which Ganesh had made were completely disjointed. He had written CIA in block letters at the beginning of the notes and had put a big question mark next to it.

Dr Balagopal had studied in the USA. But who was the westerner they had met at Connemara that day? Dr Kenneth?

Ganesh's theory was definitely a strange one. Raja was nothing but an instrument in a big project. A small cog in a big wheel of conspiracy. They had experimented with him to find out whether they could change memories fully or not. Did they use hypnotism or medicine?

The American Intelligence Agency, CIA had used 139 drugs for their Artichoke project like Adrenaline, Aktetron, Amphetamine, Caffeine, Cocaine and others. Dr Balagopal had used one of these medicines for his experiments. Why? Letter number 1131 of CIA states: 'There are two main methods of controlling human behaviour—the first is psychological and the second is pharmacological….The latter is better.' But why? What was the reason?

It might have happened as Vasanth had suggested. It was possible to change the memory temporarily by medication. Raja had been given some medicines. These had changed his memory….but why? What was the connection between Jawaahar Vittal and ICF Raja? If that one factor was ignored, would everything else fit in? Now….

The doctor who studied in the US wanted to conduct an experiment. Raja was given the medicine and his thoughts were controlled and temporarily he became Jawahar Vittal…No…it did not sound right.

Ganesh slept with the note pad on his chest. The ringing of the telephone woke him up.

"Boss, Vasanth. Have you had some sleep?"

"I went to sleep just now, Vasanth."

"Oh! Did you also have a sleepless night?"

"Are you calling from the prison?"

"No."

"Then?"

"The work is over."

"You mean...?"

"We broke into Balagopal's clinic and removed something."

"What?"

"Suspense!"

"Can I make a guess? Tape recorder? Tape? "

"No. What I took away was only information contained in a four square centimeter object."

"What is it? Why don't you tell me?"

"You just can't guess at all."

"Hey you! Out with it."

"Micro film Boss."

Vasanth arrived and showed the micro film. "A Godrej cupboard, a small locker in the cupboard, a book inside and inside that book….."

Ganesh looked at it in the sunlight. "It is very minute…Seems to be pretty difficult to read."

"I have already arranged for that. There is a micro film projector in Shastri Bhawan, in one of the government offices. There is a clerk…"

"Who has a younger sister whom you know?"

"How did you know that…..? I have already arranged for

the projection at ten o' clock. By the way, Vasantha would like to meet you. She is your fan."

"Oh god, you incorrigible man!'

"Then Boss, I have not yet given you my report on stealing. Our man Pakkiri has such deft fingers. It inspires admiration! Breaking a lock is an art, Boss."

"Ok, you entered after breaking the lock."

"Pakkiri refused to come inside. He said his job was only to break the lock. He switched on the light in the reception area and started reading a magazine. I went inside. I could hear my heart beat as loud as a banjo drum."

"Vasanth, these details are not needed. You stole and came back. Is that all?'

"Wait. You have to hear everything. It looked like a laboratory. Innumerable medicine bottles, strange machines, everything well polished, shining and new and made in the USA. There was a big EEG machine.....The place was full of machines and medicines. The National two-in-one cassette radio was the only odd thing there."

'You rascal, did you steal that also?"

"No, no. I just removed the cassette from that."

"Then... this micro film?"

"I have already told you. One Godrej cupboard, a small locker in that, inside that—Boss, Godrej is as dear to Pakkiri as his own life."

"How many more of your friends are thieves?"

"There is Mastan in Saidapet. He is an expert in climbing drain pipes."

Ganesh took the tape and looked at it.

"Have you already listened to the tape?"

"I listened but could not understand. Only plain instrumental music. But…."

"But?"

"It is strange music. Why don't you listen to it?"

Vasanth played the cassette for Ganesh.

It was mostly silent, then, all of a sudden, the music blared into a crescendo. The music was neither English, nor European, nor Russian nor South East Asian. It was a strange tune, with unexpected sudden turns. Just one or two instruments alone could be recognized.

"What music is this?"

"Who knows, Boss? There is just this one tune in the tape. Is not the music a bit strange?"

Vasanth picked up Ganesh's notes and read through them. He said, "There is nothing new in this. Your notes read almost similar to what I had already explained to you."

"There is no connection at all. ICF Raja—Peter's Road—Jawahar Vittal—Dr Balagopal of Mylapore…..Then that girl…. then the strange music. But there has to be a common factor which connects all these things. But what is it?"

"Can we see this micro film?"

The office in Shastri Bhawan was attached to the Home

Ministry. It had a magnifier to enlarge a micro film and also a printer. Ganesh was waiting outside. Vasanth came out with a printout after fifteen minutes. Ganesh stopped under the shade of a tree and glanced through the prints.

'Absolute secret. For your eyes only.'

- After choosing the target, 3 cc Epidosin-D can be given.
- Induce him into hypnotic trance.
- There are three methods by which you can test whether the target is suitable for the project. The Danikin method is the most popular of all. It involves changing his memory temporarily.

Hypnotize him for three to four sessions. During these hypnotic sessions, you have to repeatedly inculcate in his mind that 'you are not whom you claim to be but somebody else' so that it gets deeply embedded in his memory.

It is preferable if the other person is a living person. It could be you or your friend, or a friend who is already informed of this experiment, or one of your patients. Then you have to teach the chosen target that person's very personal details.

For example—You are not John but Robert. Your wife's name, you have this many children, your dog's name, where you are employed...

You have to repeat this innumerable times. If the target is suitable for us, he will change completely. He will behave like the changed person for at least fifteen days. For the target to regain his old memory, Anti doxin 323, 2 cc should be administered as IV in a supine position and he be made to sleep a couple of hours. As soon as he wakes up, he will be his old self again. Any recollection of those fifteen days would be completely erased from his memory. The person who can be changed like this easily is the most suitable person for the project.

"For what?" said Vasanth.

"I don't know, but one thing is clear. Jawahar Vittal—Raja—Balagopal are all connected. Dr Balagopal changed Raja into Vittal for fifteen days just to make sure he was suitable for the job. This is Davidson's famous method."

"Jawahar Vittal might be Balagopal's patient. Hence the personal details could be known to him. Ok, it does fit. But what does the project mean? What project?"

Ganesh shook his head in exasperation and started the car.

As Ganesh was entering his office, the telephone was ringing. He picked it up.

"Ganesh?"

"Speaking."

"Rajendran here."

"Oh hello, Rajendran!"

Rajendran smiled and said, "Since how long have you started doing such jobs?"

"What job?"

"Theft of course! Your assistant has broken into a clinic in Mylapore and stolen money."

"Money? No, not money."

"That means burglary is true and you are also aware of that.

Ganesh, why do you do such lowly work……?"

"Rajendran, how did you find out?"

"So, you think you are the only intelligent person? The police are not that bad, Ganesh!"

"Oh no! I didn't mean it that way at all."

"You think about how we might have deduced this. In the meanwhile, ask Vasanth to meet me. Has he been to prison earlier?"

"No."

"If there is no valid explanation, I will definitely send him to prison. What sort of people are you all!"

Ganesh put down the phone and stared ahead with a blank look.

Vasanth said, "What happened, Boss?"

"We have been caught by Rajendran.He says very clearly that it was you who broke into the clinic last night."

"Oh God! How did they find out?"

"He has asked you to meet him."

"Please Boss, I have never been to a prison in my life," Vasanth said with worry writ large on his face.

"We will both meet Rajendran and explain to him in detail the reason for breaking into the clinic. If he accepts our reason, well and good."

"Otherwise?"

"You stay in prison for a few days and I will meet you every day."

"See, how you let me down in times of need. How did they

find out? Surprise indeed!"

"In such burglary cases, they pick up finger prints. That Pakkiri is an established criminal. His finger prints would be known to the police force in all the districts. They would have questioned him using their own methods. He would have let the cat out of the bag by saying that it was my friend Vasanth who took me there... Vasanth..."

Ganesh almost screamed the last word.

"What happened Boss?"

"Look at the paper! Read this news. Look at it... This is the news ! Read it... read!"Ganesh looked feverish with excitement.

The news which Ganesh pointed to was published in a corner on the front page of the newspaper. Vasanth read...

'Syliana's President's visit to Chennai.'

Chennai July 4th.

Syliana's President is visiting Chennai for two days.

The first day, Friday the 6th: He will have a conference with the chief minister, followed by a dinner hosted in his honour. Saturday, he is visiting the Central Government's Integral Coach Factory. ICF has specially manufactured 100 coaches for Syliana. The President is to receive the very first coach from the Chairman of the ICF. A function is planned in this connection. Later, he is visiting the Madras Atomic Power Station at Kalpakkam. He is leaving for New Delhi at nine pm.

Ganesh said, "Syliana! Where is this Syliana?"

"South America! The newly independent nation from

Spanish rule."

"Is it not under Communist rule now?"

Vasanth whistled, "Boss, what are you implying? If our thoughts are the same, then this is a serious matter. "

"This is definitely a serious matter, Vasanth! Did it not bother us when we came to know that a man was brought all the way from ICF to Mylapore?"

Vasanth hesitated, thought for a second, then said, "It is frightening even to think about this."

"It is just a possibility only. First you have to meet Rajendran. Before we tell our crazy theory to him, we have to find out more details. What day is it today?"

"Friday."

"Don't we have time till tomorrow?"

"Yes."

"First make enquiries at ICF. Find out the details of the function, and also how, where and when it is to be held."

"I can get all the details from the Public Relations Office."

"You find out all that first, somehow or the other."

"What about this cassette?"

"Wait, wait. I have to think a little bit. Why don't you find out the details of the programme first? Can you do it or should we approach through Rajendran?"

"What are we going to tell him? Will he believe us?"

"That's precisely why I want more details, specifically, whether Raja is involved with the function in any way."

"No problem, I can find out."

"Raja is an ordinary foreman in ICF. There is no chance for him to participate when such VIP's arrive for a function. Even then, are they going to have the function in front of the workers? Or else, is it going to take place symbolically in the Management block? I want all the details."

"Boss, you have a fertile imagination."

"This is not imagination, Vasanth. We are trying to reconstruct the whole picture with whatever little facts that are available. Anyhow, why don't you go to Perambur and collect all the details?"

"Don't worry. Within the next hour and a half, you will get all the information! Can I take the car?"

"By all means! You may take it whenever you want. One more thing, Vasanth! Suppose you cannot…."

"There is nothing which cannot be done by me!"

"No Vasanth, the threatening telephone call…"

"Don't worry. Nobody can do anything to me."

An hour—two hours—three hours elapsed. No telephone call. No news from Vasanth. Ganesh became worried. The time taken to Perambur from Ganesh's office was a maximum of forty minutes. It may take an hour or two to make enquiries there. Another couple of hours lapsed. Still no news from Vasanth. Ganesh felt angry with him. 'How irresponsible is he? Does he not have the sense to inform me? I'll wait another five minutes. Then...'

The telephone rang. Thank God! Has to be Vasanth.

"Ganesh here."

"Ganesh, Rajendran here."

"Rajendran? Oh Rajendran! What is the matter?"

"MSR 6633, is it your car?"

"Yes."

"White Fiat?"

"Yes."

"Then it is your friend Vasanth..."

"What happened?" Ganesh felt fear seeping through his whole body.

"You come to the Intensive Care Unit at GH."

"What's happened Rajendran? What's happened to Vasanth?"

"On our way to Perambur, we saw your car. The door was open. A lonely place. No trace of any human being. We saw a man lying in a bush about 10 to 15 metres away. He was bashed up, his face was swollen and bloody. Multiple fractures."

"My God! Is he alive?"

"Yes, but he is critical. Ganesh, tell me what is the matter? I think you are doing something without my knowledge... You break the lock of a clinic just like a common thief! Then, this! Ganesh, What is all this?"

"I will tell you everything, Rajendran. But before that—Vasanth! I have to meet Vasanth first."

"You meet him in the hospital and come straight to the office. Is that clear? Your car is with us."

As Ganesh was going by taxi, he felt choked with emotion. 'Vasanth, my dear friend! I am extremely sorry. I have been an idiot. When the matter was so serious, how could I have sent you alone? My enemies are aware of each and every movement of mine. Their threat was real, and they meant business. Who are they? What I thought was right. This is a very serious matter. Extremely serious! However crazy it may sound, I have to inform Rajendran. Vasanth boy, I can't handle this alone. I am sorry.'

In the ICU, Vasanth was lying with his eyes closed among the various instruments. My goodness! How many bandages! A big one on his forehead, one on his chest and one on his jaw bone. Oxygen being fed through his nose. Blood transfusion through his left hand.

" Vasanth!"

"Shhh… Don't disturb."

"Is he sleeping or unconscious?"

"He is under sedation. We have given him Morphine."

Vasanth was lying with his eyes closed. Ganesh enquired of the doctor who was close by.

"We are doing our best. Don't worry. The patient is young and has good stamina. Nothing will improve by our worrying."

"Will he survive?"

"The hospital is running on that hope only."

Ganesh drove to Rajendran's office.

"My God! Ganesh!"

Rajendran was stunned. It took him sometime to talk.

"Rajendran, this is not just a possibility, but a very harsh probability. Otherwise, why should Vasanth be attacked like this? Definitely treason is being planned and executed."

"In that case, what do you want us to do? I just can't believe this! Are you reading too many detective novels?"

"If that is so, who attacked my assistant Vasanth? Rajendran, why was he beaten up black and blue without any enmity? May be what I say just now may sound crazy. Give me some more time to think about this matter. Before that what I ask for…"

"Syliana President's ICF programme? I'll ask them to give you a copy." Saying this, Rajendran lifted the telephone receiver.

In less than ten minutes, Rajeneran had the information. Evening 4 pm, arrival at the factory. 4.30pm, inspecting the factory. 5.15, Tea, followed by Welcome Speech. 5.35,Visiting Shop. 5.40, receiving the key for the first coach from a worker. 5.45, Reply by the Dignitary….. 5.50, National Anthem, Syliana, followed by National Anthem, India.

"Worker! Worker! Rajendran, who is the worker? What is his name? I want the information immediately."

"No problem! Just a minute, I'll find out and let you know." Rajendran picked up the telephone. Ganesh glanced through the programme again. 5.40, inspecting the coach with that worker! 5.45, Reply by the dignitary. 5.50 National Anthem, Syliana, National Anthem, India.

Ganesh banged the table with his fist. "That's it! That's it! Syliana's National Anthem!"

"Ganesh, what has happened to you?"

"Rajendran, I have a cassette with a song recorded on it. Can you ring up some official in the Syliana Consulate and play this cassette to verify whether it is their National Anthem?"

"Ganesh, can you tell me what exactly you have on your mind?"

"Sir, the worker, have you found out his name?"

"A foreman, Raja."

"Give me your hand, Rajendran."

"What?"

"Rajendran, the whole conspiracy is confirmed. The plan is definitely going to be carried out. The Syliana Republican President is to be assassinated tomorrow in that function.

"Was it tomorrow? But the function is today."

" Today? What day is it today?"

" Friday."

"In the paper it was announced that he was visiting ICF tomorrow."

"Don't you know that it was preponed by a day?"

"Today? If it is today—what time is it now, Rajendran?"

"4.30pm."

"Rajendran, come quickly! We have to go to Perambur immediately. If we are delayed, everything will be lost. Hurry up!"

"You wanted to find out something from the Consulate?"

"We have no time for any of those things. It is that urgent. On our way, I will tell you everything in great detail.. Let's hurry..."

He jumped into the jeep with Rajendran. The jeep shot off like an arrow released from its quiver.

"Ganesh, what is this? Can you clarify the national anthem matter?"

"Rajendran, it is like this. A foreman—Raja—is going to hand over the key to Syliana's President. Is it not so?"

"Yes!"

"He is the same Raja who was arrested in the Jawahar Vittal case and later released on bail. Dr Balagopal and company brought him to Mylapore and tested whether his mental thoughts could be changed easily. They were successful in changing Raja's mind. Why? All these things are nothing but a rehearsal for the more sinister action which is to follow later."

"Ok. That's what you said earlier also. But, what about the national anthem?"

"Both by medication as well as by hypnotism, a person can be controlled to do things like a doll which is operated by a key. I read this in a book. CIA has many methods. What sort of a doll? Just a trigger is all that is needed to make the man execute the dangerous mission etched deep in his mind," he said.

"Raja is going to do that as soon as he hears the national anthem of Syliana. The moment he hears the song, he will get into a frenzy. The violence which is deeply embedded in his mind will come to the fore. When he was hypnotized, in his sub-conscious mind, he might have been shown the Syliana President's picture repeatedly. They played the same song again and again, and instructed him constantly, "Kill him, shoot him, shoot him." All these murderous instincts are etched deep in his mind. When the national anthem is played, which is the cue, the murderous instincts will be released. Raja is going to act like a robotic machine. Is he going to shoot? Is he going to strangle? I don't know! Or is he going to take a weapon and all of a sudden hit the president on the head? Even when you arrest and question him later, he won't be able to remember anything."

When they arrived at the ICF factory's main gate, they could see the flags of both the countries fluttering in the breeze among the streamers.

"Welcome, Syliana President!"

Rajendran asked the security guard, "Has the function begun?"

"It has already started and is nearing completion."

"Is it going to be over? But it is only a quarter past five!"

"Once again, they have preponed the time."

The big dais was constructed by the employees with slotted angles, GJ pipes and the timber used to make railway coaches. Rows and rows of chairs could be seen...They could hear the sound of clapping. Ganesh and Rajendran came to the periphery of the crowd, shoved them aside and peeped through.

The I C F Chairman, the Governor, Syliana's President, some Syliana's personnel, another dignitary and finally Raja were sitting on the dais. Raja sat on a chair in the right hand corner.

Syliana's President was sitting and reading from a paper

wearing his reading glasses. He was bald. It was difficult to decipher his age. His blue suit was of very fine quality and he had a red rose pinned to the lapel of his coat. His ears and nose were big and his lips were cracked. He was reading line by line what was written in their language, and the consular personnel with him was translating it simultaneously.

"Syliana and India, to have friendly ties both in culture and in industry...

"Rajendran!"

"Your friend seems to be sitting there. Is that Raja sitting in that corner?"

"Yes! The thanksgiving speech is being read out. Just a minute or two is left for the speech to end. Can you see the loud speaker man sitting on the left hand side? We have to reach him quickly."

The place was about a hundred meters from where they were standing. They pushed aside the squatting employees roughly and moved forward.

"I thank and salute the Indian citizens and the Indian industries. I take leave of you in friendship and goodwill. Greetings."

They heard the sound of clapping by the workers.

"It's over, it's over! Next is the national anthem. Come quickly, Rajendran."

The man who was near the amplifier increased the volume. It was already attached to the tape recorder.

"Hey, you, watch where you walk! You are treading on my

toes with your shoes on."

The play button was pressed. Everybody on the dais stood up and waited for the national anthems to be played.

"Ganesh, you go and catch Raja quickly."

"There is no time, no time at all."

The tape started playing. A few seconds of silence at the beginning. Just plain ssss.........

"Quick, Rajendran, first stop the tape. Just push the stop button."

Before the Syliana national anthem could be heard, Rajendran dashed up the last few steps with the ferocity of a leopard and fell on the stop button. The recorder stopped.

"You! You! Who are you?"

Rajendran told the operator softly but in a firm voice, "Look here, don't create a commotion by screaming. Police! This music is not to be played. Orders from higher authorities. Just keep quiet."

He looked at the dais with fright writ large on his face. He gestured, "What do I do?"

The people on the dais were losing their patience, and one by one they turned to the left to see what was happening. Rajendran climbed on to the dais and murmured softly to the official in the left hand corner, "I am Deputy Commissioner of Police, Intelligence. We received the news that the national anthem was not the correct one at the last moment. Hence we had to stop the music from being played." He passed on the message to the Governor, who in turn passed it on to the Syliana consular.....

He just shrugged his shoulders, raised his brows slightly, and smiled. Then he shook hands with the governor and escorted the President to the waiting consul's vehicle bearing the CC number plate with the country's flag fluttering. He left with the President.

Another Deputy Commissioner of Police came to Rajendran and said, "What is this Rajendran, why this confusion….? Could you not have given me a call?"

"I did call you and sent a message through wireless also. I couldn't reach you. Last minute developments. Sorry."

"Intelligence people are always like this. If he had felt offended, we would have lost our jobs. You can't act arbitrarily in diplomatic matters."

The crowd was dispersing. Ganesh went near Raja and said, "Hello Raja!"

Raja gave no sign of recognition when he looked at Ganesh. He said, "Hello! I don't know who you are."

Ganesh said, "Don't you recognize me?"

"I think I have seen you somewhere, but I don't remember where."

"Whether you recognise and remember me or not, can you come with us now?"

Rajendran said, "Ganesh, can we go?"

Ganesh turned and said, "Hey, you! Bring the tape recorder and the tape."

"Sir, the tape was given by them, I…."

'Nobody said anything to you…Mister, can you come?"

"Mr Raja, can you come with us?"

"Where do you want me to come and why should I come?"

"Mr Raja, the Deputy Commissioner wants to speak with you. You don't have to feel scared at all. Let's go."

Rajendran said to the ICF Chief, "I need a separate room to conduct an experiment. Ganesh, are you ready?"

"The tape recorder is ready. Raja is ready. I need just one more thing. A photograph of the Syliana President."

Rajendran looked around.

"Hey, do you have a ladder?"

"Yes Sir, I have one."

"Ok. Climb on it and get me that picture. Quick."

"What is all this Rajendran? Are you going to arrest someone? Who is to be arrested?"

"Nobody is to be arrested. All of you leave this place. Don't crowd around here. Yes, Ganesh can we leave? Which room, Sir?"

"Go straight, it is next to the tool room. Is it for questioning?"

"Has it a power point?'

"Yes, it has. Shock treatment?"

"Don't ask too many questions."

Other than Rajendran, Ganesh, Raja and the tape recorder, nobody else was allowed in that room.

"Raja, take your seat."

Ganesh said, "Raja, keep standing."

Raja said, with his eyes expressing both fear as well as perplexity, "What are you going to do?"

"Relax, just nothing, Mr Raja. We are going to play a song for you. That's all."

Ganesh kept the photograph of the Syliana President in front of Raja. He rewound the tape. Rajendran was standing in front of Raja but slightly away from the photograph. The tape recorder's play button was pressed down firmly.. Silence.

"What are you going to do?"

"Shhh……"

All of a sudden, the Syliana National Anthem started playing. It contained the same tune and the same music recorded in the stolen tape brought by Vasanth. Ganesh watched Raja closely.

As Raja heard the music, his body became taut. The forehead narrowed in deep concentration. He bit his lips. There was a dot of blood on his lips. He closed his fists and took a deep breath. His forehead was covered with perspiration. He slowly rolled his eyes. His body turned like a robot and his eyes fell on the photograph. A sound similar to that of an animal's, emanated from deep within his throat. He attacked the photograph with his fists savagely till it got torn. The glass cover was not a hindrance to him. The wooden frame was scattered all over the place. He tore the photo into very minute pieces, and jumped and trampled on them. Then he looked around for a weapon, took a big spanner hanging from the wall. With eyes blurred,...and turning red, he hit the picture again and again.

Ganesh pressed the stop button. Raja fell on the chair completely drained. With spit foaming from his mouth, tongue hanging out, eyes half closed, he breathed heavily like an injured animal.

Rajendran opened the door and said, "Quick, call a doctor."

They left the place by 6.30 in the evening. The radio was playing music. Rajendran was sitting in the front. Both were silent.

"My God! Ganesh, the President has escaped a very serious assassination attempt. Had we been slightly delayed? My God! I am scared stiff. I have never felt like this in my entire career. That Raja! It is really very frightening even to think of such a thing!"

"Did you see a pair of scissors on the table on the dais?"

"I did notice the scissors. Before anybody could react, he might have stabbed the President multiple times. Had the music not stopped in time? Ganesh, you have prevented an international crime. Brilliant! I'll recommend your name to the commissioner….."

"No need, Rajendran. It was just plain luck. The CIA is an American intelligence agency. It is an expert in assassinating communist heads of state by following that method. There is a strong rumour going around just now that Kennedy's assassination was also one such political murder."

"Do you imply that Dr Balagopal is their man?"

"Definitely! Was he not studying in the USA? Dr Kenneth from the US has joined him recently."

"We can arrest them immediately. We can keep them under constant light for three days and splash water on their faces..."

"I don't think the truth will ever come out, Rajendran. You

can try. They are all hardened criminals."

"Let's see. Leave it to us now."

"Ask him to drive straight to Dr Balagopal's clinic."

"We are going there. I have already radio messaged to keep that area under surveillance so that nobody can escape."

"Very good. They have known Syliana President's program since three months."

"Probably, there are spies in the office itself. What about this Raja? What sort of a man is he?"

"Raja is nothing but a tool in the treason. Just like a knife, gun or spanner. Syliana's President is a communist. They thought that he would be happy to participate in a workers' function. Hence Raja was chosen."

"Yes. The program was decided upon by ICF three months earlier itself."

The news was leaked to the agency which roped in Raja, and experimented on him to find out whether he was a mentally suitable subject to carry out the task. First they conducted the experiment of temporarily changing his memory. They gave him medicines and told him all the details of Jawahar Vittal repeatedly and saw to it that these were etched deep in his memory! This is where a mistake occurred. They wanted the experiment to remain within Dr Balagopal's clinic. But that man escaped and created a ruckus."

"That is right. But how did they choose Jawahar Vittal?"

"I think Jawahar Vittal is an outsider, who is not in any way involved in the conspiracy. Probably, he is one of Dr Balagopal's patients. That's how the doctor might have known all the personal details about him."

"Go on."

"Raja escaped and created a commotion, both Vasanth and I got involved, got him released on bail, and the case against him was withdrawn. The moment he was released from the prison, he was whisked back to the clinic, given an antidote that made him Raja again. The program conducted on him proved to them that Raja was suitable for their work.

Before releasing him in the ICF colony, they had sown the seeds of the killer instinct within his mind—by administering the medicine when he was neither fully asleep nor fully awake, playing the national anthem repeatedly, keeping in front the Syliana President's photograph or a film clipping, along with the instruction through the head phone, "Kill him! kill him! strangle him! Hit him on the chest." There are official records to prove that the CIA has conducted many such experiments... The whole process takes place within the mind. That is its uniqueness. For the outside world, he is Raja. But Raja is unaware of whatever has been implanted into his memory. It will never ever come out."

"When would it come to the fore?"

"When he listened to the national anthem!"

" That' it."

"Oh my God!"

"That music was the trigger. The moment he heard the

music, the unique frenzy would seize him. Towards whom was this frenzy directed? Towards Syliana's President. He would look at the president. He would pick up whatever was available nearby and either smash his head or stab him repeatedly. You have witnessed what happened! How much violence was exhibited. You saw how he tore the President's picture into pieces. The President was to have been torn into pieces like that. Thank God, he escaped."

The jeep stopped in CP Kovil Street in Mylapore slightly ahead of Dr Balagopal's polyclinic. "Rajendran, I will go in first, you join me after a couple of minutes."

"Be careful..."

Ganesh got down from the jeep and entered the clinic cautiously. There were about ten to fifteen people waiting for their turn to meet the doctor. There were a few empty chairs also. There was no change at all. The receptionist was sitting behind the half circular table.

It was not Preeti but some other girl.

"May I help you?"

"The receptionist who was here earlier, Miss Preeti?"

"She is on leave. I am substituting for her."

"I want to meet Dr Balagopal."

"Do you have an appointment?"

He said, "No. Police."

"Sorry, Dr Balagopal is not in station. Instead ,would you like to meet Dr Chiranjeevi?"

Rajendran said, "Where is Dr Balagopal?"

"My God! Is this a raid?"

"Where is Balagpoal?"

She picked up the telephone and said, "Dr Chiranjeevi, the police are here." The door of one of the rooms opened and Dr Chiranjeevi, who was quite bald, with thick framed spectacles, and a white coat emerged and said, "Hello! Have you come in connection with the theft which took place last night in the clinic?"

"No. We are here to meet Dr Balagopal."

"But Dr Balagopal has gone abroad."

"Which country?"

"The USA."

Ganesh and Rajendran looked at each other.

"Anything serious?"

"When is he expected back?"

"Can't say. He is a visiting Professor there. I think it may take about six months."

Rajendran said, "The bird has flown away."

"Dr Kenneth?"

"He too has left. Can you tell me what the matter is? We will cooperate fully with you."

""We want to search the clinic thoroughly."

"Now?"

"Yes, of course."

"There are many patients waiting. If you could give me sometime…"

"You have one minute."

"I see! By all means! Come inside. You can search wherever and whatever you want.....Please come..."

We had let the main conspirators escape.

"Rajendran, you carry on with the search.....I am leaving."

"Ok Ganesh, come to the office in the morning."

As Ganesh was leaving, Rajendran said, "Thanks, Ganesh."

Ganesh came out and thought to himself, 'Even if you strain the clinic through a fine wire mesh strainer, you won't get any clue to the crime committed. It is nothing but a sheer waste of time and energy. They have already escaped.'

He went by an autorickshaw to Preeti's house in Teacher's colony. The house was locked. To his query the neighbours said, "The girl fainted and fell down for no apparent reason. That old lady, poor thing, she got scared. They have rushed her to the hospital. It seems that the doctors are unable to diagnose what ails her. They are all in the hospital. The mother's sisters and other relatives have come."

"Which hospital?"

"They mentioned some hospital's name!"

"Is it a private nursing home or a government hospital?"

"We don't know, sorry."

Cursing, Ganesh got into the auto. He felt that a few people had come on the stage, played their parts and disappeared without a trace.

Where is that girl? Where is Dr Balagopal? Where is Raja? Where is the President of Syliana....? Different, different, directions.

Who is real among them?

Vasanth! Yes, Vasanth's trauma alone is the present day's reality.

"Go to the General Hospital."

# Sacrifice

I MISSED my flight at Chicago's O'Hare airport. I didn't notice the tufted haired priest on the next seat. I was reading the news from the small television attached to the chair after putting the coins in the slot. I wondered how to spend the next five hours! I yawned and looked around to find the source of the sandal and camphor smell. I saw the priest sitting on the next seat. An American. But like a religious priest with a tuft. Probably, shaving only every Wednesday, wearing a dhoti made of rough cloth woven by hand and worn the traditional Indian way. The thin towel on his torso was worn like a sari. He would have fitted beautifully in the *Mannargudi Rajagopala Swamy* temple. He gave me a friendly smile. He was reading a very old Sanskrit book which had turned sandy yellow due to frequent use. He asked me for the time and I replied.

He asked me in English, "Are you from Bharat?" He didn't use the word India.

"Yes."

"Name?"

I told him my name. "Your name please."

"I am Mitchelle. That's my previous birth name. Now I am Bharadwajan."

" Iskon movement?"

"No, No. They are all phonies. We have radical thoughts and are extremists going back to the *Vedas*. Being a citizen of Bharat, you would be aware of the richness of the *Vedas—Rig, Daitriyam, Sama, Atharava Veda*.

I said, "It is not *Daitriyam* but *Yajur*."

He said, " *Daitriyam* is another name for *Yajur Veda*."

I felt a bit ashamed. "I do not know Sanskrit. I am a computer engineer. I had come to your country for training."

He smiled and said, "I am reading your country's books."

"Surprising! we have to call this a full circle. Vedas and Upanishads are no longer useful to us. You people have taken hold of them."

He looked at me with a smile and said, "You are the losers."

"No, they are not useful for the present day living. You can read, that's all."

"Who says so? In our 'Back to the Vedas' movement, we follow the Vedas in all aspects."

"Not possible."

"How can you say that without studying them?"

"I can vouch from as much as I have read. The *Vedas* are full of sacrifices and sacrifices alone."

"It is wrong to say that about all the *Vedas*. Veda means learning, intelligence, knowledge. *Rig Veda* is the various prayer songs of many Gods. *Sama Veda* is about music. *Yajur Veda* is the one that speaks about rules that you mentioned. Even in this, there are two distinct groups, two classifications—*Krishna Yajur*, and *Shukla Yajur*. *Atharva Veda* is all about magic and subjugation rituals. How many chapters has *Rig Veda*! How many hymns!"

The way he started explaining seriously brought a smile to my face. What a strange absurdity! An American priest with a tuft on his head, explaining Vedas to an Indian Brahmin who had come to America to learn computer science, sitting at O'Hare airport, in the modern age of television viewing at the drop of coins, sitting on fibre chairs.

"It is wrong to say that you cannot perform sacrifices in practice. We, in Vedapuri, perform all the sacrifices mentioned in all the forty chapters of *Vaajasa Neyi Samhita*. We also perform *Agni Hotram* and *Saadhu Masyam*."

"Vedapuri?"

"Yes. It is located forty miles from here. That is our headquarters." He asked me again what the time was. He said, "Another four and a half hours. If you are interested, I will take you there. But only if you are interested."

I thought about it. It was better than being confined in this glass cage. Let me find out what they are actually doing.

"Why do you smile?"

"I am a Brahmin. It is people like me who should perform these rituals in Indian forests. You Americans who belong to the jet age perform these on your soil."

"Wrong. Four types of priests—*Hodha, Ukkadha, Advariyu,* Brahmins came to take part in *Sraudha Yagyas.*"

Though his Americanised Sanskrit was funny, I realized that he was much, much better informed about the Vedas, than I. His eyes showed curiosity, the typical American keen interest to learn in detail about things. I didn't want to be caught on the wrong foot. I wanted to know what they were doing. I said, "Okay, I will come."

"Are you willing to take part in our *Purushmedha*?"

I said, "yes."

He said very happily, "Please come."

We came out of the airport. Since the fog had cleared, ten to fifteen planes were landing on the runway.

I could see rows and rows of cars as far as the eyes could see, till the horizon. He said, "Vedapuri is meant as an escape from all this." His car was parked half a mile away in the eighth slot. It was an ascetic orange in colour and had both BTV and *Om* written on it. Even the seat covers were the same orange. We crawled for some time, then left the expressway and entered into a narrow, deserted and quiet path. I was surprised to see such a pathway in America. The car shook with each and every movement as it entered the forest area. He talked incessantly while driving. They followed the Vedic age for both food and their living. "The ideas of *Vedas* are the best ideas for human civilization. The Big Bang Theory of today is mentioned in the *Rig Veda*. Darkness enveloped by darkness and the great deluge took place and due to penance became a single mass ..."

I said, "Our country remains backward and ruined only due to these useless books. If only these books were burnt, we would have been definitely much better placed. What we need from you is not *Vedas* but dollars!" Probably his feelings were hurt. After this he didn't speak at all but drove in silence.

After a little while, we reached a thick forest enclosure, well fenced by strong iron wire mesh. It had a board, 'Welcome to Vedapuri' and '*Suswagatham*' written both in English as well as in Sanskrit. The path narrowed still further and I could see deer leaping around. I could see thatched huts further away. I wondered how they managed to get the palm leaves. We got down and walked. I saw a quadrangular thatched place, where there was an altar in the form of a bird with spread out wings and a burning fire. A few white skinned ascetics with red beards were spooning ghee—yes ghee into the smouldering fire and chanting "*Om, Om.*"

Bharadwajan said, "*Agni Sayana Kriya*". When I looked up, American ladies in pale yellow saris were standing and five cow's heads were kept in a row in front of them. Vermillion could be seen on their foreheads and the *vedic* chants had reached a crescendo. He said, "Sacrifice to gods *Aswini* and *Indra*." He crossed the place and went to a priest under the shade of a tree and said, "Mahaprabhu, I have brought him."

The ascetic said, "Good, what is the name?" Cat's eyes, red beard. Texas type ascetic. He had a typical ascetic jug with a spout, *rudraksha* beads around his matted hair tied in a knot on his head. I was confused as to which age and country I had come to.

I said, "Sankaranarayanan."

"Brahmin?"

"Yes."

"Excellent! Pingalai, take him away."

One of the girls came near me with a smile and said, "Come with me."

Since she wore no brassiere, her juggling breasts were visible, bobbing up and down. It was soothing, whether it was the age of *Vedas* or computers. Pingalai took me to another place which was open all around, gave me a dhoti and a towel, both in red and said, "Wear these."

"Why?"

She said, "Your modern dress is not suitable for the sacrifice."

I said, "Will you help me to change into these?"

"Yes of course, why not?" So saying, she came near me and removed my shirt. As she did so, her body just grazed mine. She put a garland of yellow flowers around my neck and put a slightly elongated vermillion mark on my forehead.

I said, "What sacrifice?"

"Did not Bharadwaj tell you? You can have fruits if you are

hungry."

"No, he didn't tell me. What sacrifice?"

"*Purushamedham.*"

"What does it imply?"

She looked up and asked me, "Did not Prajapati tell you?"

"No, but why?"

"There are 184 types of *Purshamedha* sacrifices. What is to take place today is in the 30th chapter of *Yajurveda*. Are you a singer?"

"No, why?"

"Brahmin?"

"Yes."

"Understood. To achieve the status of the best among the priests, they are going to sacrifice you today."

"Wait a minute. What did you say? Human Sacrifice?"

"Yes. They are going to sacrifice you. That is what *Purushamedham* involves. *Yajurveda* has rules—sacrifice a soldier for kings, a Sudra (the lowest of the four Hindu castes) for ascetics, a thief for darkness, for lust, a prostitute, for heaven, a bald-headed man."

I said with a smile, "You must be joking."

"No." She tied my hands at the back and said, "Take him."

Six people came near me.

# City

MADURAI WAS the second capital city of the Pandya kings. The 'Madra' seen in antique maps, called 'Madura' in English, 'Medora' by the Greeks is only this Tamil Madurai.

Caldwell's *Grammar Of Comparison*.

Various advertisements in foot-high letters covered the walls. Nizam Lady Tobacco—RK Brassiers—Be warned! Revolutionary Fire!—Gospel Meetings— Hajimoosa Textile Shop (Textile Ocean)—30-09-73, the day the atheists will bear fire-pots.

An ordinary day in Madurai. As usual, the line of pots near the water-tap appeared to be doing penance for the people. Small boys were playing in the mud without any worry about tetanus. Pandyan Transport Corporation buses were emitting nationalized diesel smoke. Policemen in starched uniforms, lacking protein nourishment were controlling the chaotic human, as well as the vehicular traffic, moving hither and thither.

The city's human movements resembled a sort of 'Brownian Movement.' A khadi-clad, thin and not very long procession was crawling on the left side of the street abusing the government against the price rise. People in bare-feet and with folded-up dhotis crowded the frozen tower gateways of Meenakshi Temple and the dried-up Vaigai bridge.

Our story is about a woman who has come to the city today. Valliammal was waiting with her daughter, Pappathi, in the corridor of the OPD at Madurai's General Hospital. The previous day Pappathi had fever. The doctor at the village Primary Health Centre where she was taken frightened her saying, "Rush her to the General Hospital immediately!" She boarded an early morning bus.

Pappathi was on a stretcher. Six doctors crowded around her. She is about twelve years old. Both her nostrils were pierced and the cheap glass stones shone brightly in the hospital light. Her forehead had a streak of sacred ash. She was covered upto her chest, revealing her twig-like hands. Pappathi was in a feverish sleep. Her mouth was open.

The Chief doctor examined her by turning her head and lifting the eyelids. He pressed her cheeks with his fingers. The Chief had studied abroad. He was teaching at the Post-graduate level. Professor! Those who were with him were his medical students.

"Acute case of Meningitis. Notice the....."

Valliammal was looking at her daughter with anxiety and worry without understanding the conversation among the doctors. Those who were around came one by one and looked through the opthalmoscope into Pappathi's eyes. They tested whether the eyes were moving by flashing the torch light. They jotted down notes.

The Chief said, "Get her admitted."

Valliammal looked at each of them by turn. One of them said, "Look here Mother, this girl has to be admitted in the hospital immediately. Can you see the man sitting over there? Go to him. Where is the chit?"

Valliammal did not have the chit.

"It's alright. He will give you one. You, the old man, come over here."

Valliammal looked at the Chief doctor and asked him, "Sir, will the child be alright?"

"First, you admit her. We will take care. Dr Danasekaran, I myself will attend to this case. See that she is admitted. I have to take my class. When I return, I'll examine her."

He left like a minister with a retinue of followers. Dr Danasekaran instructed Srinivasan, who was present there and then swiftly followed the Chief.

Srinivasan looked at Valliammal.

"Come here Mother. What is your name? Hey! You! Useless fellow! Take out the register."

"Valliammal."

"Patient's name?"

"He is dead."

Srinivasan looked up.

"Patient means the sick person.....Who is to be admitted?"

"My daughter."

"What is her name?"

" Valliammal."

"Are you being funny? What is your daughter's name?"

"Pappathi."

"Pappathi. Lord be praised!"

"Take this chit straight to the man sitting on a chair near the staircase. He checks the income. Give this to him."

"The child?"

"Nothing will happen to the child. Let her lie here just like this. Has nobody come with you? You go and come back. Who is Vijayaraghavan?"

Valliammal didn't want to leave Pappathi. The long queue and the smell were nauseating. She felt angry with her dead husband.

She took the chit and went. The chair was empty. The back of the chair was dirty. She showed the chit to the man nearby. He gave the chit a cursory glance and said, "Wait. Let him come," and pointed to the empty chair. Valliammal felt a very strong urge to go back to her daughter. To her unlettered mind, the magnitude of the question whether to wait or go back to her daughter seemed to expand to the size of the universe.

She felt diffident to ask the question, "Will it take a long time?"

The person to assess the income came leisurely after getting his nephew admitted in the hospital. He took his seat. He became brisk after touching his nose three times with snuff and brushing it off with a handkerchief rolled like a rope.

"Look here. Stand in a queue. If you crowd around me like winged white-ants, what can I do?"

Valliammal had to wait for thirty minutes for her turn. Then her chit was pulled from her hands unceremoniously.

"Get the doctor's signature. Doctor's signature is not there at all."

"Where have I to go for that?"

"Where have you come from?"

"From Moonandipatti."

The clerk said *hath* and laughed.

"Moonandipatti! Bring back the chit."

She gave back the chit. He turned it this way and that way like a fan.

"How much does your husband earn?"

"My husband is no more."

"What is your income?"

She stared without any comprehension.

"How many rupees do you earn per month?"

"When I go for harvesting, I am paid in kind as paddy, besides ragi and millets."

"No cash? It's alright. I'll enter as ninety rupees."

"Per month?"

"Don't be scared. They won't charge you anything. Look here, take this chit, go straight and then turn left. There will be an arrow mark on the wall. Go to room no 48."

Valliammal took the chit with both her hands. The directions which the clerk gave confused her simple mind and she roamed all over the hospital like a piece of paper blown about freely in a gust of wind. She was illiterate. The number forty-eight had immediately receded from her memory. She was afraid to go back to the clerk and ask again.

Two patients on a single stretcher, sitting and half reclining with a tube inserted in their noses crossed her. A trolley with sambar-rice filled upto the brim in a wide mouthed vessel crossed her slowly. White caps were seen. Well-groomed lady doctors in white coats and stethoscopes decorating their necks like a garland were moving around. Policemen, people with coffee tumblers, and nurses were all walking in different directions. They were all in a hurry. It didn't strike her to stop any one of them and ask for guidance. She had no idea what to ask either. There was a big crowd in front of a nondescript room. A man was collecting many straw coloured chits just like the one she had. She gave her chit also. He took the chit without paying any attention. Everybody was waiting on the bench outside. Valliammal became anxious about Pappathi. The girl was all alone there. The man who collected the chits called out the names one by one and made them sit in a queue. When Pappathi's turn came, he saw the chit, returned it and said, "You brought this here! Take this back. Go straight." Valliammal said, "Sir, I don't know where this place is." He thought for a second, then stopped a man passing by and said, "Amalraj, take this woman to forty-eight." He turned to Valliammal and said, "Follow this man. He is going there."

She had to run after Amalraj to keep pace with him.

There, another crowd was waiting on another bench. Valliammal hadn't eaten since the morning and the smells of the hospital made her dizzy.

She was called after half-an-hour. She entered the room. Two men were sitting facing each other, and were writing with a pencil. One of them glanced at her chit. He turned it and looked at it. He held it in a slanting position and peered at it.

"Are you coming from the OPD?"

She couldn't answer this question.

"It is written 'for admission'. Just now there is no vacancy. You come tomorrow morning sharp at half past seven. Is that clear?"

"Where have I to come, sir?"

"Come straight here itself. Is that clear?"

The moment she came out of the room, Valliammal's anxiety about her daughter Pappathi, whom she had left unattended for almost an hour and a half, greatly increased. She didn't know the way to return to her daughter. All the hospital rooms looked alike. The same man seemed to be sitting again and again in different rooms. One ward had many people with plastered limbs in traction. In another, a row of small children with knitted brows were crying. She was at a loss where to turn in the maze of corridors, machines, patients and doctors.

"Madam," she called a lady doctor and told her from where she had set out. "A group of doctors were discussing. They asked about the income and said no need to pay anything. Madam, I have left my child there."

She followed the way the doctor guided her to find the door to the gate locked. At once, her fear turned into panic. She started weeping. She stood right in the middle of the corridor and shed copious tears. A man asked her to stand aside and weep. Her crying in that place seemed to be the normal occurrence similar to the aseptic smell of the hospital. She walked away saying, "Pappathi! Pappathi! Where will I see you? Where do I go?" She saw a door, somewhere. An exit to go outside the hospital. The gate was open. It was manned only to let people leave the hospital. She remembered having seen it.

She came outside. She recollected that she had walked a long distance from there before entering the hospital through another gate. She remembered the wooden stairs. The chairs occupied by the income assessors were vacant. At last!

But, the gate was closed. She could see Pappathi still lying on the stretcher with her eyes closed.

"Sir, please open the gate. My daughter is there."

"You come sharp at three. Now everything is closed." She pleaded with him in humble tones for ten minutes in vain. Though he spoke Tamil only, she could not make out what he said. She failed to understand his query. He opened the gate to somebody else in exchange of a small consideration which he accepted with great reverence by touching it to his eyes. She barged in against his protests. She lifted her daughter in a tight embrace with relief and sat alone on a bench and cried piteously.

The Chief had a cup of coffee after his lecture for the MD students and went to the ward. He clearly remembered the Meningitis case of the morning. Very recently, he had read about a few new medicines for the disease.

"Where is the Meningitis case I had asked to admit in the morning? Twelve-year-old girl. Where is she?"

"Nobody was admitted today, Doctor."

"What? No admission? I had left specific instructions. Don't you remember, Danasekaran?"

"Yes, I do remember, Doctor."

"Paul, go and find out what happened. How could it be missed?"

Paul went straight down and asked the clerks sitting opposite each other.

"What is this? You people send notes, "admit, admit" just like that. There is no place for a foothold in the ward."

"Respected sir! This is a query from the Chief."

"Are they known to him?"

" May be. How do I know?"

"Twelve-year-old girl didn't come this side at all. Even if somebody else had come, I had asked them all to come tomorrow morning at half-past seven. Two or three beds will become vacant by tonight. In case of an emergency, don't you have to inform earlier? Just a simple word that the Chief is interested in the case. Relatives?"

Valliammal didn't know what she was going to do till 7.30 the next morning. The hospital atmosphere frightened her very much. She wondered whether they would let her stay with her daughter. She thought about this for sometime. She gathered Pappathi in both her arms. She held her against her chest, like a small baby of six months, with the head sloping at an incline on the shoulder and hands and legs dangling by the side. She came out of the hospital. She hired a cycle- rickshaw and directed him to go to the bus stand.

"What nonsense? Tomorrow morning at 7.30? But the girl will die before that. Dr Danasekaran, you go and check in the OPD. They will be there. If there is no wretched bed in this ward, there is a bed in our department ward itself. See to it that this is allotted. Quick!"

"Doctor, but that is reserved!"

"I don't care. I want that girl admitted now. Right now!"

The Chief had never ever thundered like this before. Frightened beyond belief, Dr Danasekaran, Paul, Chief nurse Miranda and everybody ran looking for Valliammal in the OPD.

"Is this not a simple fever? Let's go back to Moonandipatti itself. We will consult the village doctor. No need to go to the village hospital. That hospital doctor frightened me and sent me to Madurai. You will get well soon. We will offer the white, sacred, hardened ash ball to the village deity and use the sacred ash which is enchanted by recitation of prayers."

The cycle rickshaw was going towards the bus terminus. Valliammal took a vow and prayed that she would offer a handful of coins to Vaideeswaran temple if Pappathi got cured!

# The Edge

I DECIDED to kill Vijay. This was not a decision taken on the spur of the moment. I thought and debated about this for many days. This thought kept churning in my mind without respite. I tried to quell it by smoking endless number of cigarettes and crushing them before reaching this decision. I felt greatly relieved after it was taken. The sense of relief was similar to the one which one gets after a good body massage.

There is no hurry at all. I am going to take my own time to think and plan how to kill him. I ponder on why I have chosen to kill Vijay. I don't like him at all. It is as simple as that. There are so many things in this world which I don't like. I don't like him in the least. The reason?

The reason lies in my history. We have to go back to my younger days. The way I grew up, was shaped up, my qualifications, all these be told to you. Can you listen to me with patience?

Don't call me insane. I am an introvert. Just a simple stare from you is enough for me to get back into my shell and keep my distance. I won't trouble you. If you want a part in murdering Vijay, don't speak. Just listen to me. Don't interfere. Listen to me fully and decide for yourself whether my decision is right or wrong.

First, about me. I am Sarathy. Twenty-eight years old. According to the horoscope, my birth star is Ashwini. Zodiac sign, Aries. When I was three years old, an incident took place which is deeply etched in my memory.

Both my parents are standing facing each other. I stand in between on the bed staring without understanding what is happening. My father is screaming at the top of his voice. The nerves on his neck stand out like wriggling worms. His face is red due to his ferocity. My mother is standing and crying in front of him. I cannot understand the reason. It is just a memory block. I don't understand why this memory is etched in my mind till today. My mind holds many such unrelated blocks like this. Each and every block resembles unconnected islands. These are similar to haemoglobin spots which you see in the blood through a microscope.

Why did my mother cry that day? Why did my father scream like that making his nerves swell up? The next memory about my father is of bamboo! green bamboos, coconut palm leaves, white sheet, the toes tied with a piece of cloth. Open mouth, unshaved face with small prickly hair, a pot of cold water poured on me, a lone drum, a mud pot with fire held by coir rope, smoke, my mother who was helped up to the street.

Mother didn't cry!

Why?—was another question.

I don't want to burden you by telling you too many of my personal afflictions and be told, "Oh, you poor thing."

Both Vijay and I are working in the same office. I get many opportunities to kill him there. I have not yet decided whether to kill him there or at home. I have to think about this.

In the beginning, Vijay and I were friends. That too, very close friends. I can tell you precisely when we parted ways. What a close friendship we had in the beginning! I have unburdened my inner mental anguish and sought consolation from him. I have confided my dreams to him. My fears, my strange dilemmas, my strong aversion to the many events happening in this world. I have a very strong aversion to people who tell lies. If anybody tells lies intentionally, I feel like slapping them, whether it is my wife or a stranger in the street. I feel terribly agitated when I come across falsehood. Do you know how I have struggled to control this anger? We tell so many lies in our day to day life. A shopkeeper denies having change for five rupees, though he has enough change. Newspapers report untruths. Radio, cinema—all tell lies and nothing but lies. Thinking about this for many days, I doubt whether 'truth' actually exists in this world. All the actions of this world seem to depend on varying degrees of lies only. They say that there is a God. That is the only truth. I had thought that all the other things were false. One day I wrote a letter to God—an inland letter. Don't feel surprised. I posted the letter after writing it. The address:

Respected God

That's all. Is He not omnipresent? Does He require any other address?

I think that letter might have reached Him. What I had written in that is the following:

Every day I have doubts. This happens frequently. Hence, as soon as you receive this letter, send a reply to the following address

JV Sarathy

No 18, 3rd Stage, 4th Block

West off Chord Road

Bangalore 560040

Writing a letter to God! What rubbish! But I received a reply. Yes, I still possess that reply.

Place: Everything

Time: Always

Dear Mr JVSarathy,

Received your letter. Thank you. Does not the very fact that you have received a reply to your letter prove that I exist? Don't be confused. Blessings!

With love,

God.

Beautiful, well-rounded handwriting. I was satisfied and

wondered how I received this letter. I looked at the post office seal, Bangalore-1. Was it not appropriate that the letter reached the head post office?

How appropriately Kamban has declared, "Oh Lord, we take refuge with you."

There is another thing about this letter to God. I will mention it later.

I can't say clearly when this desire to kill sprouted within me. Also, I don't know when I chose Vijay as my prey. Since the past two years, my health has not been good. My losing interest in many things was the first symptom of this disease. Normally, I sleep till half-past-six in the morning. All of a sudden I developed sleeplessness. I used to wake up by three-thirty in the night. There was confusion about where I was. My wife would be lying next to me. Who was she? What was the relationship between us? Was she my co-traveller in the everlasting journey of this human life? Suddenly I used to feel frightened. What would happen to me after death? When they cremated my body after weeping inconsolably, would my memory alone remain? Oh my God! It is burning. You wretched people! It is burning! Please, pull me out… Fears of this kind. I read books on death for that whole month. Memory is small, tiny chemical and electrical whirls within the mind. When blood stops flowing into the brain, the whirls become dysfunctional. Death is a permanent full stop. After that just plain darkness. A deep cut. That is all. This is the viewpoint of one group of people. Another group says death is a continuing action. It is nothing but casting off your robes, floating in the open space and donning another robe.

By the Christian doctrine, death is waiting for the Last Judgement of God, buried and frozen underground .... *Quran* also says the same thing ... who is right and who is wrong among them? ... I cannot understand. I have stopped thinking about this. Since the last few days, I have started looking at my reflection in the mirror. For hours and hours together, at my own reflection. With hesitation, I have started looking at myself in any mirror which I come across without being conscious about it, be it the bathroom mirror or the small square one which is used to comb the hair, or those which you come across occasionally in the streets. Why? I am not a handsome man. My height is only 5 ft 3 inches, that too with my boots on. I only reach up to my forehead in many mirrors. How can I explain the strangeness of the reflection in the full length mirror which is entirely different from me? It seems like looking at a stranger. I used to scrutinize, very carefully. Hair, small forehead, thick eyebrows, triangular shaped face, listless eyes, hair which springs untidily, protruding teeth ... In the bathroom, climbing up on the stool after shedding all the clothes, I used to examine myself. This body is not mine ... Somebody else's. Somebody else's clothes given to me temporarily. I thought that the reflection in front of me possessed an entirely different system of its own. I felt that the reflection would remain there even when I moved away.

I suffered from constipation for a few days. For two to three days my stomach was as heavy as a rock and it got cured only by taking the light brown powder mixed with warm water given by the doctor. Is it possible to take this every day? The trouble started again when I stopped … I wondered whether there was any connection between my mental attitude and this problem. Whenever my mind was vexed, the trouble also made its presence felt. I used to get angry for very minor things and would remain without talking to my wife. For one or two weeks, the answers used to be just monosyllables. When I thought about my wife, at times I could feel the urge rising in me. My mother married me off as soon as I landed a job. It is my mother who brought me up. My father's memory is restricted only to the two reflections which I have mentioned earlier. My mother brought me up by working in various houses, her only ambition being my welfare and my achieving higher goals. She sacrificed good food, new clothes for herself to provide for her son. My eyes become moist when I think about my mother.

Jayalakshmi was chosen by my mother. I used to repeat this again and again to her. I used to tell her that she had to thank my mother for her marriage to me. In the new flush of marriage, why, even on my wedding night, I was speaking to her only about my mother. I have spoken to her for hours and hours and days and days together about my mother only. Once she said, "You are obsessed with your mother." I didn't speak to her for a week.

My wife is as tall as me. Her hair is curly and thick but not soft. I have never seen her without the red dot on her forehead.

She is the sixth daughter from a poor family. She used to tuck in her sari and finish all the household work very quickly. Her preparation of *upma* is very different. There are no lumps at all. The cashewnuts shine like gold in the *upma*. It has a special flavour of its own. But it cannot be equated with my mother's. What my mother used to make was a different kind of nectar. After preparing any dish, Jaya would always ask ,"Does it taste like your mother's?" I would shake my head in the negative and say, "Another mother is to be born for that."

Both my mother and Jayalakshmi competed with each other in my mind. In this, my wife's winning showed my weakness. My mother stayed with us when we were married. I suffered a lot in those days. My mother used to sleep in the hall while I used to lie down with Jayalakshmi in the bedroom. I used to push Jaya away when she tried to spread herself on me, with a pang of guilt. I felt it was a great sin to indulge in such lowly acts when my mother was sleeping there. Have you read the autobiography of Gandhi? I suffered like that. Then the household work! I used to get angry if I saw my mother sweeping the hall. I used to rebuke her, "Is Jaya not there? Why do you do all the work? Hey Jaya… Do you think this is funny?"

"Your mother only offered to do the sweeping."

"Don't say 'your mother'. She is like a mother to you also."

But she could not think like that at all. It became the root cause of friction between the two of us. When I returned from the office both would be standing in two different corners. I used to stand helplessly between them. I used to pounce upon my wife. She would weep. This happened every day—I used to go and sit in the park, unable to tolerate it. These incidents are narrated to you so that you can understand and observe the reasons for my mind having turned ugly.

Finally, my mother herself found a solution to this dilemma. "Sarathy! I am in good health. I have decided to go and stay in our house in the village as long as my health is good. I'll return when I can't manage. Jayalakshmi is a good girl. But my presence here causes some friction. You have inherited my stubbornness. My leaving this place is good for everybody. When you get a child, I'll return and take care of it. For the present, it is better that I live separately. I am not angry at all. Don't keep on frightening her for no reason at all."

I almost wept while I pleaded with her. "Don't go mother." But she stubbornly refused to stay back.

Her leaving left a void which is not easy to explain. Why Jaya could not understand an ideal person like my mother? Was she that stupid? Cruel? I was so angry with her that I didn't even bother to register her presence for a whole month. But this wretched physical body! Her breathing could be heard in the darkness next to me! How soft she was! The savage force which exists in this world, since time immemorial, setting aside all humane feelings was my downfall.

I used to write letters regularly every week. I visited my mother whenever there was an opportunity. I pleaded with her repeatedly,

"Mother, please come back." She would say March, then April, then May but she would not come.

She left me permanently due to an attack of jaundice. I was unable to control my emotions.

She was gone! I had nobody. My wife could not reach my inner self. This sorrow is one which will endure till my death. My mother who brought me up single handedly without a husband! Her death left a deep scar on me. She started appearing in my dreams—almost everyday. Then only the truth struck me—she was not dead, she was within me. When I looked into the mirror, I could see my reflection dissolving into that of my mother.

Then this matter about Vijay. Hey Vijay! My hands are throbbing to kill you. Why? I will tell you. I am not justifying my actions and I am definitely not going to waver from my decision. The fairness and foulness of this action is irrelevant to me.

I met Vijay for the first time six months after my mother's death. The moment I saw him, I liked him. He was holding a cup of coffee and reading the newspaper, sitting at the table.

I said, "I am Sarathy."

"Hello, I am Vijay."

I said, "You are reading the newspaper during office hours!"

"Don't be formal. We are friends. All the work entrusted to me is complete. All the reports are ready. Hence, I am reading. If I have work for eight hours I will work for all eight hours without a break."

"I liked you the moment I saw you."

"Thanks. I have to understand you better to say those same words to you."

"Where is everybody?"

"They all left for lunch a bit earlier … I don't do that."

I sat down saying, "Good habit." We were alone. I looked at Vijay pensively for some time.

"Why do you look at me like that?"

"I was wondering whether I could speak to you about myself."

"That's for you to decide."

"Will you keep this as a secret?"

"I will listen and then decide that."

"Mr Vijay."

"Just Vijay, please!"

"Vijay, of late, my inner thoughts completely overpower me. I no longer have any interest, desire or care for anything in life."

He laughed saying, "Probably indigestion."

"The problem is with my mind, not my stomach."

"Sorry, don't be angry, go ahead."

"Do you want me to tell you from the beginning?"

"Lunch break is half an hour! Tell me what you can before they all return. You can tell me the rest tomorrow."

I confided in him not just that day but for many days. I told him everything from the beginning to the end. My birth, growing up, how my mother brought me up, my marriage, my mother's death, my fears, my thoughts about death, the strange habit of looking into the mirror, loss of patience, no interest in anything, the doubts and fears about not having a child till now! About my wife, the writing of a letter to God. One day, Vijay offered me a lighted cigarette. He inhaled deeply and started thinking.

"You have to meet a doctor, immediately."

"I have already met him and taken medicine for constipation!"

"Not that doctor. A psychiatrist—the one who deals with mental disorders.... Wait." He opened the telephone directory, "Mmmm let's see. National Highways, National Industries... National Institute of Mental Health and Neuroscience! Hosur Road, Bangalore—24. Do you know where it is? If you go to LalBagh gate by Double Road, you can locate the Department of Psychiatry. You go there the first thing tomorrow."

"Do you mean to say I am mad?"

"No, I didn't mean that. But you must not get these sort of thoughts—its abnormal. I feel you are on the edge of something. We are on this side. A deep, bottomless chasm is on the other side. It is better that you meet him before you jump into the chasm. Can I ring him up?"

"No, no... I'll go on my own."

"You can't be trusted. I'll call him. It is best at this stage. Don't be scared. You tell the doctor whatever you have told me. They are ali good doctors and are there to help people like you."

I looked at Vijay as he diallied. I was greatly touched by his interest in me! I experienced a new found interest. What he says is right. I needed psychiatric help.

The institute was a separate building by itself. The Bangalore milk dairy across the street reminded me of my mother. I got down from the bus and walked.

Very, very tall trees, long corridor, Clinical Psychology, Neurology, Neurosurgery, Theuro Anaesthesis... How many different departments! How many people! Are all these people insane? But they are behaving normally!

The serene atmosphere of that place made me feel calm. A young doctor asked me, "Doctor's name?"

I had a blank look and said, "This is my first visit. Vijay rang Dr Chandrasekar."

"Dr Vijay?"

"No, Vijay is not a doctor, but my friend."

"Dr Chandrasekar?"

"Yes."

"You want to meet Dr Chandrasekar? Wait, what is your name?"

"Sarathy."

"Age?"

"Thirty."

Short and pointed questions. The form had four sides. He filled it up as I was answering. "What is your trouble?"

"My thoughts!"

"Can you explain in detail?"

"Don't I have to repeat the whole thing again to Dr Chandrsekar?" The man stared at me, tore the sheet with a swift movement and said, "You go straight to room no 86. It is on the first floor."

There was a picture of Eugen Bleuler, the Swiss psychiatrist with a goatee. Dr Chandrasekar was sitting behind the table beside a pristine, white pleated curtain. He had a big nose and penetrating eyes behind flat and broad spectacles. He looked at the card and said in a soft voice, "Sit down Mr Sarathy. Tell me about your trouble."

I said, "Depression, doctor."

He looked at the card again and said, "Depression is a very general term. Tell me in detail." He answered the telephone which rang, with a smile. I waited. I wanted to tell him everything. I wondered where to begin.

"Are you confused about how and where to begin? Ok, I'll ask the questions. You say, depression? Where did you read that word?"

"In a book."

"Which book?"

"A book on psychiatry."

"Oh! Interesting. Why did you read that book?"

"I was confused about what was happening to me. I had a desire to read all about the mind. I think I suffer from a manic depressive state. Paranoid."

He smiled and said, "The first thing, throw away all those books. As if your own imagination is not enough! We are the people to read all these books. A layman will get confused unnecessarily. Tell me, do you read anything else other than psychiatry?"

"A bit of Theology. A little about philosophy, about God."

"That's interesting." He noted that down. "According to you, who is God?"

"A woman, my mother!"

"Is that so, Mr Sarathy? Can you remember clearly any one of your recent dreams?"

"You get dreams only when you sleep."

"Don't you sleep at all?"

"My thoughts drive me crazy, doctor."

"What sort of thoughts?"

"The thoughts of ten men."

"Have you read about Chekhov?"

"No, why?"

"He said, 'I dream the dreams of ten men.' Don't you remember even a single one of your dreams?"

"I remember just one."

"Tell me…"

"There is a big bridge, no, a dam. On this side, the water which is harnessed is making ripples. I peep into it. The water is a hundred or hundred and fifty feet deep. There is a road along the embankment of the dam. The parapet wall is as tall as my hip. I walk on the parapet wall instead of the road. Balancing just like a circus artist."

"I see! Do you get this dream again and again?"

"I can't say. But I remember this dream very clearly."

"Did you ever fall into the water at anytime?"

"No, I keep walking."

"Sarathy, how is your eyesight, your general health?"

"My eyesight is normal. I have got my eyes tested. I suffer from constipation and indigestion frequently."

He opened a book, "What is your impression of this picture?"

"Is this not a Rorschach picture?"

"Don't worry about that. Forget all that you have read in the psychiatry books. What is your impression of this picture?"

I said, "A moustached man is gazing at the sky. On his chest he has two eyes and a nose..."

"This?"

He showed some ink blotted pictures. I told him whatever I felt. He tested my reflexes. Asked me to write. Showed different coloured dotted paintings, checked my blood pressure and heart beat. Talked a lot.

"Did you write a letter to God?"

"Yes. I received a reply also, doctor. I am a deeply religious person. I used to go to the temple with my mother. I used to pray and touch with reverence all the nine planets. I used to go to all the temples, Shaiva or Vaihsnava, and also churches. Sometimes I used to feel scared suddenly. Was it wrong to have cremated my mother? I used to feel that she was calling me saying, 'Son I am still alive, don't burn me….' Oh my God! I didn't give her an opportunity to rise and come out. I used to cry the whole night thinking about what I had done …"

I cried.

He admonished, "Mr Sarathy, what is this?"

He waited till I composed myself. "Do you smoke?"

"occasionally."

"Any drugs?"

"No."

"Who all are in the house?"

"Me and my wife, that's all. No children."

"Does your wife know about your visit to this institution?"

"No. Only Vijay knows."

"Who is Vijay?"

"The one who called you, my friend. He is my colleague in the office."

"Why did you not bring him?"

"He only boosted my confidence and asked me to come here alone."

He prescribed some medicines on a sheet and said, "You take these medicines at night. Can you spend a week here as an in-patient? Is that convenient for you? Where do you stay?"

"Rajaji Nagar."

"Can you come and stay here with your wife."

"Why doctor? Am I mentally unbalanced?"

"No, no! But it is preferable to take a short treatment for a week as an in-patient. Don't be scared. An injection is to be taken daily. That is all.

"Insulin shock?"

"Look here, I have already told you to forget all that you have read. But you have to spend a week here definitely. Preferably, get admitted tomorrow itself."

"Why don't you prescribe the injection... I'll get it injected by a doctor nearby."

"It's not like that. The reaction is to be observed. It's better that you remain as an in-patient. Will you come?"

"These tablets?"

"Just plain sleeping tablets. You might have taken some on your own."

"I have taken only some tranquilizers. Librium ..."

"Just leave out everything. Come tomorrow at the same time. Okay? There is nothing wrong with you. You are alright."

"Doctor, why don't you say that I am normal?"

"Alright, normal! Can you bring the reply from God when you come tomorrow?"

"Definitely ."

As I was returning by auto-rickshaw, I thought deeply about the doctor's reaction to me. If I am normal, why admit me as an in-patient in a mental hospital? Why an injection every day? I had spoken a lot with him. Was there anything wrong with what I had said? No, probably he detected something wrong with my mental equilibrium, hence, I needed some psychiatric treatment. What the heck! It was wrong to have gone there. Now how do I tell this to my wife? If I have to get admitted in the mental hospital tomorrow, she will start imagining things... These specialists are rotten. Rascals. What is wrong if the injection can be arranged at home. This proves the injection is not an ordinary one. Shock. Electricity. No, but some strong anaesthetic medicines. No, I am not going there. What is wrong with me? Nothing. My mother is alive. She will be reborn as my child. She is going to take divine incarnation. If I can't get her through my wife, I'll force all other women and get her through one of them. This is a divine secret. Vijay met me during the lunch break. He asked, "Did you go?"

"Mmm..."

"What did he say? He is supposed to be a renowned doctor."

" The doctor said that I have to get admitted in the hospital."

"Good. Fine. Take leave of absence. Get admitted and be relaxed."

"I am not going there."

"Why?"

"Nothing is wrong with me. He said I was normal."

"Then why did he suggest that you get admitted?"

"Why, you tell me."

"Sarathy! Don't be stubborn. He knows what he is talking about. Why don't you listen to him?"

"I am definitely not going."

"Don't be stupid."

"He is stupid. Why should he ask a normal person to get admitted?"

"He might have said normal, without meaning it, so that you

won't feel scared. You are not normal."

"Then why would the doctor tell a lie? I don't like lies."

Vijay got angry. "Look, something is definitely, terribly wrong with you. He alone can treat you. You must go there positively."

"Jaya will be scared."

"I'll tell her, convince her."

"Who are you to talk to my wife?"

"There you go again." Vijay's hands trembled. He filled a glass with water and drank. I left the place.

"Sarathy, don't go. I have to tell you something."

"What is it?"

"I am worried about you, Sarathy! Do you remember the letter that you wrote to God?"

"Yes. The doctor has asked me to bring the reply."

"Do you know who wrote the reply? Me. You idiot, it was only me. As if God will reply to any letter. That was my handwriting…."

I was shocked and said, "You wretch."

"Listen to this also. Do you remember what all you have told me about yourself? Probably you don't remember anything. The thoughts of your younger days, the way your mother brought you up, your neighbours… Did you say all this to the doctor?"

"Mmm..."

"From all the incidents that you have narrated, one thing is very clear to me! Have you noticed that?"

"What is it?"

"Shall I tell you? Can you bear it?"

"Say it! Say it! I am normal. I can bear anything."

"The way your mother lived! My dear Sarathy, kindle your memories again. Dig out the thought which is deeply embedded in your memory. You were mentioning Raju! Who is Raju? Why did he visit every week? Sarathy, try and recollect clearly. The toy monkey, which walked when wound. The toy which hopped, making a *chirk chirk* noise. Who gave you that? Raju uncle! You played with it always. You lost it one day and went looking for it. You went into the bedroom quietly without making any noise. What did you see?"

I closed my ears. "Oh God! Don't say anything. Don't say anything. I didn't see anything. Stop Vijay, stop."

"From where did you get the money for your education? How did you get the new boots? How did the money come to the hostel every month regularly without fail? How Sarathy? How?"

"Don't say anything. Stop! Stop! What you say is absolute rubbish and nonsense. Please Vijay, don't speak any further. Stop! Don't confuse me. Don't spoil the only perfect picture within me. You are an evil person with perverted ideas. That's why you are thinking like this."

He laughed saying, "I am speaking the truth...Then on Ram Navami day...."

"Are you going to stop now or shall I kill you?"

"Look Sarathy, you can kill me, but you can't kill your thoughts. Go. Go back home! Go to the hospital tomorrow itself positively. Launder all your thoughts clean. Make your mind like a pristine white curtain. Destroy all the red Rorschach pictures. Search for peace. Hurry up! Take leave of absence, and run!"

I ran. Vijay's mocking laughter could be heard inside my head. All that he said was lies. What sort of a perverted person is he? Trying to poison my mind by narrating this sort of gossip. … What sort of sadist is he? Is there any truth in what he says? He is just blabbering. Cruel man! The wretch! Pervert! I should not have spoken to him at all. How bad a person was he to imply such perverted ideas! He wants to destroy me completely. My telling him about the letter to God and his ridiculing me by sending a reply to it reveals his true nature as a mean person. Dr Chandrasekar had his doubts about my mental balance when he was informed about the letter. I don't want anything to do with Vijay at all. I don't want to talk to him at all. No need to have a smoke or coffee in his company. But what to do with him? How can I let him live after the way he has slandered my mother? I have to finish him off. I should have strangled him to death then and there itself! Wait, Wait! Think calmly. No need for any hurry. I have to kill him by planning meticulously. Be patient and cautious.

I came home. Jaya woke up from her afternoon nap. She looked at me fearfully and asked, "Why have you come early, are you not well?"

I said, "I'm ok." I went straight into the bathroom. I looked at my face in the bathroom mirror for a few minutes. My face changed. First the moustache and the beard grew, eyes sank deep into their sockets and shrunk into the skull only to transform into a flaxen haired baby with chubby cheeks and lovely eyes, full of life…

Mother! This is my duty. I have to do this. This slaying is essential, to establish the principles as well as the truth I firmly believe in. To destroy falsehood, the only option left for me is to kill Vijay.

Jaya knocked on the bathroom door.

Be careful. Nobody is to know about my decision. I have to behave like a normal person to the outside world. I opened the door after washing and wiping my face with a towel. I said, "What is it?"

"Thank god. I was scared. What is the matter? Why were you perspiring so profusely??"

"There's nothing wrong with me, Jaya. Can I have a cup of coffee?"

"I'll make it just now."

"Come, let's go to the cinema and be happy."

She looked at me as if seeing me for the first time.

"Jaya ! Have I not acted strangely with you many times?"

"You treat me any way you like, but please talk to me. What tortures me the most is when you sit quietly for hours and hours, and days and days without talking."

"I won't behave like that again, Jaya. We can have coffee outside. Just get dressed."

She ran inside with new found happiness.

How am I different from the others? I behaved just like any normal husband. I walked with her upto the bus stand, giving up the one available seat to her, getting the tickets. Standing in the queue at the cinema for balcony seats, purchased popcorn for her, enjoyed all the advertisements shown on the screen .... How can I be called abnormal! That rascal doctor is telling lies. Vijay... I don't want to think about that wretched sinner!

The film was all about love. The music was loud and noisy. At one stage, my attention was diverted from the film. I saw the Rorschach picture playing on the screen. I closed my eyes.

She shook me saying, "Don't you like the film? Shall we go?"

I said, "No." It was intermission. I went to the restroom. I looked at the mirror and was shocked to see Vijay standing in the queue. I turned around and pretended that I hadn't seen him. He had come on his own.

He said, " Hello, Sarathy."

I didn't answer him. What is this, why won't he leave me alone?

"Are you angry with me because I asked you that question?."

I didn't answer him.

"I thought about it after you left. Sarathy, it was wrong on my part to have said those things. I felt very bad afterwards. I could not work in the office. I left after taking permission. I just entered the theatre to see this film. It was my good fortune that I saw you here so that I could apologize to you."

I didn't answer him at all.

"Sarathy, will you never ever talk to me?"

How dare he? He had destroyed my mind completely. Planted a poisonous seed within it and now asks me why I am angry with him and whether I won't talk to him. 'Vijay! Yes, I am angry! You are going to be punished for your action. Death sentence—beware.'

When I returned to my seat, the film had begun. A film started in my mind also. My mind too replayed the visuals uttered by him in the morning. The words transformed themselves into colours, first black then a dirty brown and started oozing out all over my mind. In a corner of my mind, a devil peeped out and wondered whether there could be any truth in what he said. The other part said that it was very wrong even to think like that. My wife synchronized with the celluloid figures and cried, laughed and shuddered. I also cried, laughed and shuddered in my own personal film.

We had coffee and snacks in a hotel in Ananda Rao circle. My wife was very happy. She said, "Please remain like this always."

Days! How many more days are left to kill Vijjayan? Then? I will be arrested.

Death sentence? Life imprisonment?

She said, "Can I ask you something?"

"What is it?"

"Somebody from your office said something?"

I was alarmed and asked, "Who and what?"

"Natesan."

Thank God! Its Natesan and not Vijay! I sighed in relief. "What did he say?"

"People in your office are going to Nandi Hills for a picnic this coming Saturday."

" Yes, so?"

"Can we join them?"

I felt a sense of elation all of a sudden. Picnic! Nandi Hill! Vijay also would be there. Yes. There I'd get many opportunities to finish him off.

"Jaya, a good idea! We will definitely go. I will ask them to include our names also tomorrow itself. We have not gone on a picnic like this, happily, since a long time ...

She pressed my hand joyfully.

I was thinking about Nandi Hills as we were returning home. I had been there once about five years back. A tall hill ... a big bungalow. A lone hotel. Tipu's drop..... The peak which slopes down suddenly to a deep gorge. I felt happy. An unexpected opportunity given by God. Though he didn't reply to my letter with his own hands, he has answered me indirectly. He has proved his presence by arranging this favourable situation. Oh God, you are definitely great!.

I could not sleep that night even after taking the tablets. Vijay's words were reverberating in my mind.

"How did you get the money for your education? How did you get the new boots? How did you get money in the hostel regularly, without fail? Sarathy, how?

"Don't say anything. Stop, Stop!"

"I'll definitely say these things. I'll repeat again and again. Shall I ask you something? That day you returned home failing to get a ticket for the film!"

"No, please don't say anything! I beg of you."

My wife shook me to wakefulness. "What happened? Did you have an unpleasant dream?"

"No!"

"Here, have some water."

I could have no peace of mind as long as Vijay was alive, even if I remained without talking to him till the end of my days! Just seeing him makes me lose my patience. How dared he, the scoundrel? What right had he to talk like this? No, he has to die definitely. I have to kill him first before I do anything else. Dear Nandi Hills! Here I come! Oh my dear hills, you are going to liberate me, I'm coming. I have decided to kill him, definitely! All my mental torture will end when Vijay is finished. Is it necessary that I will be caught? I can escape, if I plan meticulously. The plan is to be executed with a lot of deliberation, and without anybody suspecting me.

My conscience is not going to prick me after I kill Vijay. I am not going to feel guilty at all. He is the devil who possessed me and rattled my mind. I'll be happy thinking 'good riddance.' I do not need a doctor, or injections or medicines of any sort. Vijay has to be finished off. I'll finish him off …

Later, I slept peacefully.

The next day, the moment I reached the office, I gave both my name as well as my wife's for the picnic. Then I told Natesan casually, "Natesan, let me have a look at the list of names."

"Why?"

"Just to have an idea, who all are coming."

I saw the list. Vijay's name was also there. Thank God! I returned to my seat. Will Natesan remember what I asked him just now? No, No! Don't feel scared. What is wrong in asking who all are coming on the trip? That's a natural query. Sarathy don't be scared, don't be scared.

Vijay came again to me in the afternoon. I pretended to be engrossed in my files and ignored him.

"What? Still angry with me?"

I didn't answer.

"When will you talk to me? At least let me know that."

I stared at him, with fire in my eyes.

He laughed and said, "You may burn me to death by that look, Sarathy. People tend to get angry when the truth is told."

"Get out."

"I'll leave. But think about what I said in a calm manner. Even now, it is not too late. You may go to the doctor tomorrow. He will tell you what is best for you. He will erase everything."

"Vijay, I am definitely going to erase everything."

"You seem to have given your name for the picnic … very good. Will you talk to me there at least or are you going to sulk? Will you introduce your wife to me?" Saying this, he laughed.

I am going to introduce you to something, but not my wife.

We left for Nandi Hills at nine in the morning. Thirty-five people from the office had come. Everyone was happy. Transistors were blaring. I too was a part of the childish exuberance but only superficially. My wife brought a lot of eatables—rice mixed with spices, chocolates, cookies, coffee, juice. I was sitting next to her. Vijay was sitting next to me by the window and looking outside.

Many hallis like Kanganahalli, Devanahalli passed us and I browsed through the newspaper. An article titled *Independence* caught my attention.

'We lose our independence the moment we are born. The place we are born, country, family, parents, wife are all decided at that time itself, hence, where is the independence?'

Vijay said, "What are you reading?"

"Can't you see?"

"Thank God you have spoken. "

"Wait, I'm going to speak, Vijay, I'm going to speak a lot."

My wife was talking to me non-stop. "Looking back, it is five years since we have gone anywhere like this. Thank heavens! It is almost two years since we have spoken to each other with such gay abandon."

Jaya, how am I to tell you that this is the last day for you to talk to me with so much happiness? How will she face the news? That her husband committed a murder!...No, no! Who is going to catch me? I am going to execute this after planning meticulously, so that nobody will suspect me. I said, "Jaya, don't worry I will alwayas talk to you much more and also happily."

Her face caressed my shoulder as she leaned against me. Vijay gazed outside.

The two humps of Nandi Hills could be seen at a distance. The bus strained to climb up. 'Hair pin bends', 'sound horn,' 'no overtaking,' 3800 feet, 4000 feet. We reached the entrance to Tipu Sultan's fort. Tickets were purchased. Some people had tender coconut water. "Jaya, do you want a coconut?" For a split second, the paring of the coconut reminded me of Vijay's head.

A school bus with children in uniform came and halted there. The children were happy and made a lot of noise. All of us climbed up the stairs talking among ourselves. Plenty of shaded slopes, short trees which seemed to invite even old people to climb them. The horse stables of Sultan's days, canon holes ... a statue of a bull right in the middle, a hotel with glass windows, at the peak of the hill with fantastic views, Gabban House. An antique temple.

A traditional picnic on thick sheets spread out under the shade of the trees ... eating heartily...playing cards...laughing... chasing each other...dancing to the music...playing and singing.

Lowly people! Mean people! Me? I'm great! I am going to execute a great deed from a great height!

I said, " Vijay, I want to speak to you, alone."He looked at me and said, "Thank God! The ice is broken. Speak to me."

"No, not here, but alone.Can you come with me?"

"By all means."

"Jaya, you take rest here. I am going to walk with my friend for a while."

"What, let her also come."

"No, Jaya, you stay here. You can see everyone playing some games. Join them."

Vijay smiled. "You want me to come alone with you. You want to tell me something. You are very angry. Is that so?"

"No, no."

We both walked along the gently sloping steps. We were quiet for sometime.

"What is this, why are you not talking?"

"Vijay, I thought about what you said."

"What did I say?"

"The doubt which you pointed out. It is deeply embedded in my mind like a poisonous seed. I need your help to pluck it out. I have lost my sleep. I am completely swallowed up by that disastrous incident."

"That is precisely why I suggested a remedy for it. Get yourself admitted in the hospital. They will send you back after thoroughly cleaning you."

"No, I have thought of a different method."

"There is no other alternative method for this."

"Yes, there is another one, positively, Vijay."

"What is it?"

"Don't be in a hurry, come with me…"

We climed up. Jacaranda trees were in full bloom, with mauve flowers, sans leaves. I asked a passer-by, "Where is Tipu's drop?"

He answered, "Go straight." We climbed down the incline slowly.

"Where are we going?"

"To an excellent place to speak in confidence."

I had made up my mind. Tipu's Drop was an unexpectedly steep incline. The place designated by the Sultan to punish the guilty. That's where I am going to kill him.

We climbed down carefully. The hill supported the fort wall. It had a semi-circular ring with waist high square cuts. I went there and peeped out. Down below.... I could see the road resembling a green vein. There was a sloping rock with a perpendicular fall of a thousand feet. My feet felt an itching sensation. I sat in between the edges. The breeze gently kissed me. "Vijay, look. What a beautiful place. Come and sit here beside me."

He sat with some hesitation.

"Did you bring me here to speak about the beauty of nature?"

Many scribbles could be seen on the lime mortared walls—names and numbers. Everybody wants to mark their names. A small place in history, including me.

"Vijay, look at this open space. Look below! Feel the air! How pure it is. Look at the village which is far below.... The houses look like toy houses, human beings resemble just plain dots...cars wriggle like worms...... From this elevated height, it is obvious that human life is nothing but just a speck. Even in that speck, there are distinctions like good and bad, virtuous and sinful deeds! We have to give up everything to purify all the sinful and evil thoughts arising in our mind. You too wash your dirty feelings in this open space. Come Vijay!"

"What are you saying."

"Vijay, I'll tell you clearly in simple words. You have planted a thorn in my mind. The only way for me to remove the thorn is to kill you. Your death alone will wipe out the thought. Otherwise, whenever I see you, I will be reminded of the doubt which you have sown within me. I can't possibly live with that fire raging within my mind. So you have to die."

"Hey Sarathy! what is this? What are you blabbering?"

"Vijay, this is the punishment awarded to you by me in my private court, under special jurisdiction. Get lost, you devil!"

I held him tightly and made him climb up along with me to the edge.

"Hey you! Hey Sarathy! Please! Think again. What you are doing is wrong. Whatever I said was all in jest. No Sarathy, leave me. Hey! leave me!"

"No Vijay, you have to die. This moment was already predetermined when you were born."

He held onto me with a strong, vice like grip. "Sarathy, no, I am scared. Please."

"Nothing will happen. A swim in the big open space. Then a single breaking sound. You will die within a second. Before your mind can register the pain, your brain will be smashed to pieces. Don't be afraid. Goodbye Vijay."

In a violent fit of rage, I shook him and pushed him away from me.

"Oh my God! What is this? The rascal has dragged me also down with him. Hey Vijay let go of me! You fool, you have avenged me." Both Vijay and I fell into the deep gorge, stuck together. I could hear the hissing sound of the air around me. ... second by second, the earth was in a hurry to meet us. I don't know whether the blood gushed into my brain but we both fell very very quickly...

P S Nandi Hills police outpost received a message, transmitted by a VHF radio from a small room near the temple on the hill. A police jeep arrived and people who had gone on the picnic, local people and the police searched all over the rocky ground. They found blood stains on a rock. Some people took courage and climbed further down to locate the smashed body and were shocked...

The Inspector said, "Move, move away. Is this man, a member of your party?"

"Yes Sir."

"What's the name?"

"Vijaysarthy."

# Rice

I DON'T agree with the statement that all car mechanics are cheats because there are exceptions to the rule. Unfortunately, my mechanic belongs to the general category. My car, which was running without any hiccups, started to protest by making strange noises all of a sudden. The mechanic who attended to the car pronounced in a sober tone, "Sir, the suspension is down," after taking the car for a trial run.

Though an engineer by profession, my field is different. My knowledge about automobiles can be written on the back of a bus ticket. To be honest, I have no idea where the suspension of the car is located. I didn't want to reveal my ignorance to the mechanic and replied in a knowledgable manner, "In that case, replace it."

Immediately, the man disappeared under the car after spreading a gunny bag. He asked me from under the car, "What about the kit? Will you buy that or shall I buy it for you?"

"Where is it available?"

"JC Road."

"Oh! Is that so? In that case, you do one thing! Give me an estimate of all the repairs to be done."

"How is that possible? I have to check the whole car before giving an estimate."

"Check the car properly and give an estimate."

As he was busy checking the car, I came out of the workshop. When I turned back to see what was happening, I saw the front wheels lying on the ground and various other parts too.

I felt anxious about the outcome. I realised that he was going to charge me a hefty bill by quoting fifty or a hundred rupees for each and every part to be replaced. What would happen if there was some noise while driving? I came out of the workshop cursing myself for courting this unnecessary trouble.

The workshop was at the corner of the street at the junction between Mill Corner and Central theater. It was ten in the morning. The traffic was fairly heavy. Many cars were plying on the road with healthy suspensions. I had a cup of coffee in the nearby restaurent and as I was returning to my sacrificial altar, I witnessed the accident.

An old man was coming from the Central theater side on his old ricketty cycle. An orange coloured van was coming from the main road. The old man turned the corner without thinking, unaware of the danger lurking ahead. He went straight across the van's path. It happened so suddenly that the driver was not given any time to apply the break. I just heard a big "Bang!" I didn't see the old man at all after that. I sensed the fear rolling into a ball in the pit of my stomach.

A crowd gathered at that place in no time at all. I wanted to know what had happened but hesitated. Then I moved closer to the accident site. The van had knocked down the old man and stopped. The cycle was completely crushed and resembled a fried *pappad*.

The old man was lying on the road on his side. He was bleeding from the head injury which he had received due to the accident. His mouth was open and his body was jerking. The old man was alive but his life was ebbing away very quickly.

Would you like to know how we, the citizens......honourable and responsible citizens of Bangalore behaved? Let me tell you!

"Where is the driver?"

"He is sitting there."

"But I am not the driver."

"The man is dying. Lift him up."

"Don't touch him. Let the police come."

"Stop the autorickshaw."

The auto which had stopped, gently touching the periphery of the crowd, picked up speed and flew away. The BTS bus which crossed at that moment had curious onlookers peeping through the windows. You could hear, "Prasanna, come quickly and see this," from somewhere inside the bus.

"Don't do anything till the police comes."

"Make a phone call."

"Sir, why don't you call the police?"

"I have some urgent work to attend to. The police will arrive soon."

The old man had stopped twitching. As he was breathing heavily through his mouth, air bubbles could be seen bursting out with the oozing blood.

"Who is the man?"

"Who knows?"

"Was he alone or was anybody with him?"

Somebody asked me, "Sir, please go to the hotel across the street and call the police."

With a sense of responsibility, I went to the hotel to make the phone call.

People were having their breakfast in a carefree and happy mood.

"I want to make a phone call."

"Seventy five paise."

"I'll give you."

"First you make the payment and no STD calls."

"I have to make a phone call to the police. An accident."

"No problem. You can make the call."

"What is the police emergency number?"

"I don't know."

"Don't you have a directory?"

"No."

"That man, the accident victim, is dying."

"Sir, can I give you some advice?Don't get yourself involved in this."

"What?"

"Don't get involved in any accident case. Once I took an accident victim to the hospital in my car. In the hospital they said, 'Why did you bring him here? It is a medico legal case... only Victoria Hospital attends to such cases.' You know how far away Victoria is. When I went there, they said, 'How can you bring the body alone without the police?' They made me wait for an hour- and- a- half in a corner. Then they made numerous calls and finally the police came. They snapped at me saying, 'How can you bring the body without informing us first?' When they finally admitted the case in the hospital the man was dead. They closed the case saying 'Dead on arrival,' signed the report and sent the body to the mortuary. Do you think the story ended with that? No! I was the sole witness. They made me run around the court for six months......I'd get summons.....I would go to the court.If the inspector was present, the government lawyer wouldn't turn up. If the government lawyer came, then the inspector wouldn't be there. If they both turned up, then it would be the turn of the driver's lawyer to plead for an adjournment.

"I was curious to know how much I had spent on all this and realised that it was almost a thousand rupees. Do you think it stopped with that? The case? The lawyer manipulated the questions in such a way that I was made to look like the person responsible for the accident. I just wanted to get out of the mess at any cost. The situation was really and truly very bad. All this for what? Because I did my duty as a responsible citizen...."

I listened to him wonderstruck and said, "But the police are to be informed by somebody or other."

"Of course you can call the police and be a witness to the accident if called for. I have warned you by telling you what happened to me."

"I don't know the number."

"Dial 100."

I returned to the accident site after informing the police over the phone. I saw two police constables marking the place with a chalk. As soon as I reached there, a man pointed to me and said, "This is the man."

I said, "I have informed the police."

"The police have come. Seshadripuram police station is close by. The driver went there and brought the police."

The police inspector looked at me and said, "Come here."

I went near him with some trepidation and hesitation.

"Did you see the accident?"

"Mmm...Yes, I saw the accident."

"Your name?" A diary came out of his pocket. Immediately, my dormant cautious instincts came to the fore and made me retort, "Why?"

"Why? ......Witness Sir! Witness! Did you not see the

accident?"

"Yes... I saw it, but I was not near enough. I was quite far away to see properly."

"Just now you said you saw the accident. Give me your address."

"Address? I am new to the city."

"New to the city? Don't you live in Bangalore?"

"I am from Madras."

"Ok. Don't you work here?"

"No...in fact, I am returning by Brindavan today."

He didn't believe what I said. He looked at me with a look of sympathy as well as regret.

"Sir, are you scared to be a witness?"

"Oh no! It's definitely not so. If I am not going to be in the city, how can I be a witness? Besides, this man also saw the accident."

"Oh! no I didn't see anything. I came just now."

"Won't anybody be a witness?... Anybody who has seen the accident?" The inspector asked the crowd in a helpless manner.

The crowd melted away slowly.

As a gesture to placate the inspector, I said, "Inspector, in fact I can be a witness and I have no problem or issues about that. But I am not from this city. How can I come from Madras?..."

The inspector snapped at me in anger. "You!...get lost...get lost to Madras...Why do you stand here? Go away......." He went to the old man who was dead by now.

I waited for sometime there itself. I spoke to the man standing next to me, justifying my action, "Tell me, is it possible to come all the way from Madras as a witness?"

He gave me his support and said, "How is it possible to come all the way from Madras as a witness?"

I came back to the mechanic's workshop. He was evaluating the worn out and soiled parts of my car.

He said, "The clutch plate is also worn out. Can I change it?"

I replied in the affirmative.

"The engine has to be taken out. It will take three days."

"Ok, do it. Give me an estimate."

"The total amount is three hundred and fifty. I will give you a bill for everything."

"Okay."

"Your address?"

I gave him my address.

"Since how long are you in the factory?"

"Nine years."

"Come by Wednesday."

I came out saying, "Okay."

The orange coloured van was not there. The crowd had also dispersed. There were hardly one or two people at the accident site. Even the police were not there.

I had to cross the accident site again. There were blood clots on the ground as a witness to where the old man had fallen. The cycle was also there. It was almost as old as the old man himself.

A dirty bag was hanging from the handle bar. It contained about half a kilo of rice probably purchased by the old man. The rice had spilled on the street. Half of it had fallen on the blood. Two young boys were picking up the rice grains unsoiled by blood and pocketing them hurriedly.

# Vision

THAT DAY, the first class compartment of Brindavan Express from Bangalore to Chennai was not crowded. The rush was on the opposite side where horse racing was taking place. I could see a few heads on seats similar to ones you find in an aircraft. A few people were walking up and down to while away the time. Young men with Hardly Chase novels in one hand and sporting big round sunglasses surveyed the young girls. The train had just started moving. The battalion of vendors selling coffee, jalebis in plastic satchets, chocolates, ice creams, and *masala vadas* would descend only after the train crossed Cantonment station.

I don't read books in trains. It takes five hours to reach Chennai. I like to observe people and listen to them. There did not seem to be much chance for that today. How do I while away my time? I was worried. At cantonment,the train stopped.

I didn't notice the person who came and sat on the next seat. I was observing an old Anglo Indian couple. The old man planted a routine kiss on his Rosy and quickly got into the train. She blew her nose and waved her handkerchief saying, "Bye, bye."

"How much?"

"Give me whatever you want Sir, give me something extra."

"Periyasami, how much is this? Is this a rupee?"

"Yes sir."

"Is there anybody next to me?"

"Yes sir."

"On the right side ?"

"Yes sir."

"Okay. You go to your seat. Where is your seat?"

"It is just across. The train is not at all crowded."

The conversation taking place near me was unusual. I turned to find a young man nearby, a porter in front and a nine -year-old boy in a corner.

The porter accepted the one rupee coin with gratitude, touched his eyes with it, saluted, and took leave telling the boy to take good care of his master. The young man was about twenty-five years old and had dark glasses on. Looking straight ahead, he pocketed his purse carefully. He was fair, had his hair cropped in the latest trend of fashion and his shirt was of good quality.

The young man was visually impaired. He turned slowly and tentatively and asked, "Are you also going to Madras?"

I said, "Yes."

He said, "I am Krishna Kumar and I am blind," and smiled. I was completely taken aback by this simple but striking and abrupt self introduction and wondered how to react. Should I say, "I am sorry" or "Is it so?"I told him my name with some hesitation.

He said, "Glad to meet you," and shook my hand. He continued, "It will take five hours."He had a good voice. He would make a good singer. I looked at him carefully. Watch on his wrist. Why? Clean, expensive clothes. Feet which had not done much walking. Affluent. The way he sat suggested that there was no expectation at all. He just wanted life to move in the normal course.

The train picked up speed. A non-descriptive station disappeared in a quick blur. I was keen to know more about him. The first of the battalion of the snack vendors arrived. Wafers and biscuits made a fleeting appearance under my nose. The boy—Periyasami—who accompanied him was sitting on the cushioned seat with a guilty expression. His shirt was crumpled. A safety pin substituted for a lost button. Probably, the servant boy.

The young man started the conversation. "Do you live in Bangalore?"

"Yes. Since the last three years."

He said in well articulated English, "Excuse me, am I disturbing you?"

I said "No, not at all."

"Probably you are reading something. I speak slightly more than the others. Chatting is my recreation….."

I replied, "I understand."Inappropriate words? I continued, "You can speak as much as you like. I am a good listener. I don't have any books to read. I need good company to while away the time."

"A slightly different company. Is it not so? With your permission, can I say something about you?"

"Beg pardon?"

"I have not seen you. I can't see you. I shook your hand and heard your voice. Your hands are soft. They are not the hands of a person doing manual work. Perhaps you are working in an office. Your voice indicates that you may be about thirty- five."

I replied, "Absolutely right, I am thirty- eight." He had come very close to the correct age.

"Also, I think you smoke cigarettes. There is a slight trace of cigarette smell near you."

"Remarkable! You should be in the police."

He smiled and said, "As a sniffer dog?"

"May I say just one thing about you?"

"Tell me," he said with interest.

"Even though you can't see, you don't like others to sympathize about it."

"How do you say that?"

"When the porter told your servant, 'Take good care of your master', your expression changed slightly."

He said in a soft voice barely audible, "Yes, correct. I don't like sympathy."

'My guess is not as good as yours. It is easier to guess by

observing than doing it without seeing."

"Are you a lawyer?"

"No, Engineer… Electronics."

"Where do you work?"

"Bharat Electronics."

"There is a Tamil writer in your organization."

"I know. I know him rather intimately."

"Is that you?" Very smart indeed! From the way I said, "I know him rather intimately," he quickly jumped to the conclusion.

I said "Yes."He was silent for a few minutes staring in my direction. I wondered whether he really wanted to see me somehow or other.

"I am very happy to have met you." 'Met you', the words used by the world which can see.

"May I touch you?"

I was shocked. His hands came very slowly towards me and caressed my face up and down. My hair bristled.

"I have read your stories. I liked some of them…Some are just trash. You are capable of some good writing."

"Is that so? How did you read them?"

His face clouded slightly. "Sorry, when I said that I have read your stories, I meant that I have listened to the stories read out by somebody else for me. Is not my world three quarters of the normal world?"

"Are you a graduate?"

"Yes, I have done my Masters."

"Very good."

"The June 8 *Indian Express* carried a four line snippet about me."

"Is that so?"

"Everybody was surprised. I was given an enthusiastic reception, garlanded and received an ovation. They had light refreshments too."

"Surprising indeed."

"Is it not amazing?"Did I detect a hint of mockery in his tone?

"How did you write your examination?"

"As a special case, an individual was permitted to write what I dictated. I studied by listening. I passed just by listening."

"Remarkable. MA... Which subject?"

"Political Science."

"What do you propose to do now?"

"What have I done so far to think of what to do now?"

"Why not? Till now you have done your Masters.....Now what?"

"I can study some more. That's all. If I study further, it would be Philology. I would like to study about languages. But somehow, I am tired of all these things."

"Why?"

"This MA is a privilege given to me by the world which can see. A tape recorder was allowed inside the class room... A separate writing method was set up for me... Why all these? Just to show me off in a cruel and unfeeling way to the rest of the mankind which can see. "Lo and behold! A surprise! A blind man has passed his M A examination. Garland him. Publish his name in a newspaper. Just like a two headed goat. An MA pass blind man."

He had a smile on his face when he said all this.

"I can detect a trace of disgust in your voice."

"No disgust at all. Just plain and simple truth." He sat straight. "Sir, I am born blind. I don't know the concept of vision at all. You are a writer. Can you answer just a single question of mine?"

"Yes, what is it?"

"What is colour? Can you describe colour to me? I will listen to you. What is colour?"

I remained silent. I could frame umpteen words in my mind in a wave like motion. All words recognized by eyes.

"Please tell me."

"I have to think a little."

"I am prepared to wait," he said with the same smile.

How to describe to a man who has never seen the sky since birth, who has not seen the magic hue of the evening sun, who has neither seen a girl's eyes, nor the greenery of the paddy fields, the soil's red colour—dirt, which is black—blood or flowers. Science speaks about colours in Angström units. Is it possible to kindle the dead ophthalmic nerves by numbers or words?

I made an attempt.

"Do you like music?"

"Yes, of course, lots."

"Music has seven notes, does it not?"

"Yes."

"Colours are also similar to music. Let's assume colours as music felt through sight. Violet—sa, indigo—re, blue—ga, green—ma, yellow—pa, orange—dha, red—ni. You can think along these lines. What I see outside the train's window is ma ma... pa pa ...dha dha...ni...ma...When you look up at the sky, there is a very wide *gandharam*. In the evening, some *nishadam* and *daivadham* in the west."

I looked for an echo of my thoughts as well as a response on his face.

"You explain this in a different and novel manner. I cannot understand. Try to imagine your world from that of mine. For me, train is a noise. When you sit, movements and vibrations... Travelling from one set of noises and voices to another set of noises and voices, the smell of paint, cigarette smell and the pleasant scent of flowers...."

"I can understand."

"My dreams are voices. My God is a sweet voice."

"The colours are also different voices."

"My friends are my finger's perceptions, either gentle or harsh to the touch...scents...."

"Krishna Kumar, though you cannot see, your sense of perception is much greater than that of a person with vision .You can describe your thoughts very precisely and accurately. This is definitely a gift."

"A small compensation for being blind."

We spoke about a few other things for a while. I got down at Katpadi station and strolled for a little while. The push cart book stall had books of Stanley Gardner and Siddhar's poems. I bought two oranges. A blind beggar walked along the train holding on to the window bars and implored, "Sir, I am blind, help me, please."

The young man took a rupee note carefully from his purse, located the tin container from the direction of the voice, pushed the note inside and said, "It is a rupee note! Hold on to it carefully." While the beggar blessed his progeny, the young man held his hand and pressed it in companionship.

Is it 80 miles between Katpadi and Chennai? I can never forget these eighty miles in my life. Krishna Kumar talked about himself, softly, as if talking to himself... Some excerpts... "I think with great conviction that I can remember my mother. Like a quilt as soft as feather, a very gentle, folding perception which envelops completely. She died as soon as I was born. Whatever the others said about her, I have stored in my memory. A mother who belonged to the epic age. A chaste wife, who washed her husband's feet, who fanned him, was the last to go to bed and the first to wake up....who had seen just two or three rooms all her life...... My father had hired a nanny to take care of me through the day and night and brought me up with great care. The nanny used to pinch me. This memory is still fresh in my mind. She used to smell of garlic. My father smelt of Channel 22.

"I had my meals at a specified time, had my bath, groomed myself by combing my hair, and applied talcum powder and grew up healthy. It seems I started to speak quite early. I was sent to the special school for the blind at a very early stage.

"My first introduction to Braille was through sister Clarissa's aseptic smell. The clean feeling of her starched garb, in contrast to the cotton like softness of her palms… more than that, the gentleness of her voice, when she called 'Krishna' very softly… the one who showed me the exactness of the universe for the first time. Very recently, I travelled the two hundred miles to my old school to meet sister Clarissa. She had reached eternal glory. My father had helped me at each and every step of my progress. He met the Director of Public Instruction and received special permission for me to write the final exam in the school, made me study in a college, sent me by car and, bought a tape recorder for me, arranged a poor boy to read to me, helped me to develop an interest in music, saw to it that I attended music concerts in various theatres. Very soon R Krishna Kumar became an MA—a Master of Arts.

Master of bloody blind arts.

"My father is very proud of me. He is very eager to send me to USA but I am not interested. What is America? Different perceptions and different noises across the seas. My father wants me to do LLB and practice law in a court of justice on an equal footing with the others. If I argue in court successfully, his 'mission' would culminate successfully…He would atone for his sins. Though I was born with a small defect he brought me up without any flaws. People say that I look smart and handsome with my dark glasses on. Perhaps a girl may be willing to marry me. Sex is what I have perceived occasionally through my fingers. If I had asked for it, my father would have arranged that also. My darling dad!

"I have become intelligent. Is that not enough? Great intelligence indeed!

"My life could have been worse than that of a beggar. God has saved me from a situation like the beggar who was on the platform. Am I not partially lucky to be born blind to a rich man? What do you say?"

I replied, "Your father's courage needs a word of appreciation in this situation. You have to be grateful to him also."

"For what? For having given money?"

"No—for having given you a good education. He brought you up in the normal way. To have given you permission to enter into the world of intellectuals. To have educated you with a strong will against all odds."

"Sir, I feel the greatest punishment for me in this world is my education. My father could have stopped me at the primary level, fed me in time and made me sit on a chair comfortably. That life appears to me a happier one."

"I don't follow."

"I read. I read a lot. The result? Questions and more questions without answers. What is colour? What is the sun? What is the sky? You call something beautiful. What is beauty? How can I get answers to all of them? If I don't get answers to all these questions, it is perfectly alright. In my personal, stupid world, I can form small, answers especially suitable for me. I have formed these answers... but, but...the intelligence and education which I have received, helped me to get the correct answer for my one question.

"I would not have asked this question, had I not been educated. It would not have struck me to ask these questions at all. Because I was educated, chasing after the answer, I met my old relatives. Met doctors, read books. My mother's relatives, old servants, why even this trip to Bangalore was the last pages of the odyssey in search of the answer."

"What is the question?"

"Why was I born blind?"

"What answer did you get?"

"It is because of my praiseworthy father who infected my mother with syphilis. For him? Just three shots of penicillin. For me?... Darkness, even after birth."

"Sir, we have arrived at Central. Your father has come to welcome you."

# Jillu

OUTSIDE THE window, just a lone black cloud could be seen on the horizon. Atma closed the door. It is coming. It is confirmed. By their forecast, the rain would arrive by the evening. Have to leave before that.

He turned and saw Nitya stuffing clothes into the suitcase. "Nitya, quick!"

"What to take and what to leave?"

"All told, just 8 kgs for the three of us. Take only the most essential things."

"Which are the essential things?"

Atma did not have any answer to the question at this juncture. He remembered Thoreau's *Walden*. Nothing is required of course. They can make new things in the new place.

He glanced at the living room with a pang of longing. The

various things like paintings and other collector's items which they had collected through their fifteen years of married life. The objects and articles which gave happiness, comfort and bonhomie to their life. The stereo speakers stood mute on the left and right. The attached cassette deck player, microphone, hours and hours of music frozen in colourful jackets—Beethoven, Bach, Hariprasad Chaurasia .... Nothing is required just now. A typewriter was kept close by. Is this the time to type out a poem? The cupboard was full of books. I can take something. But, which one? Research on *Tolkappiyam*? *Mukkudar Pallu*? Thiruppathis of Pandya kingdom? (all ancient Tamil literature). New poems? Four essays? Research papers on rural Tamil Nadu literature? *Paalaiyum Vazhaiyum* (Desert and Bananas). Bible? *Thirukkural*?

Which one? All these are nothing but just plain sounds. Mere sounds. The routine every day recreation and entertainment is hurling bombs, burning roofs, massacre of women and children and old people. Their daily hobby!

"Bastards." He cursed some unknown people.

"Which book to take?"

"Take something to read during the journey."

"Which one? Tell me quickly."

Atma once again fingered the cupboard. He picked up *Rani* and threw it into the box saying, "This will do."

"What to do with my jewellery box?"

"Wear everything and come. We can sell them and buy tapioca there."

Nitya looked at him with slight apprehension. "I have taken three sets of clothes for each of us. I have taken a sweater for Kumar."

"What is this big packet?"

"Our wedding album. I cannot part with this."

Atma opened it. A slim Atma and a doll like Nitya. He felt a happy contented smile within his mind. "I shivered when I touched you first."

Nitya said without paying attention. "There aren't enough locks. I have just four locks."

"Lock? For what?"

"Don't we have to lock the house?"

Atma laughed, clapped his hands and said, "You mad woman, no need to lock. There is nobody to steal anything. Whatever is there in this house—fridge, radio, TV, books, guitar, chair, toy elephant, all will remain here and here alone, even after hundreds of years, shining in alpha and beta dust particles."

Nitya remained silent for a few minutes and said, "Atma, where are we going?"

"Who knows? They say it is the Arabian Sea, Minicoy, Laccadive Islands. They will take us somewhere against the wind."

"Have we to go to Bombay first?"

"Bombay?... you stupid! ... Bombay has disappeared.... Giant mushroom! Nobody is there now. Madras? Gone! Delhi? Gone! Calcutta? Gone! ... We came here on transfer. Escaped! We can keep running away as the rain chases us. Lucky!"

Nitya asked, "Is this supposed to be our good fortune?"

"Good question but I don't know the answer. Where is Kumar?"

"He is playing outside. Kumar?"

Kumar came happily inside and said, "Dad, Dad, seven helicopters! Come and see them."

Atma came to the balcony with his son. He saw the mechanical insects landing on the ground with their rotor blades rotating and making the noise. ... *Padappadappada*... and the stabilizer's screetching sound.

"Nitya they have come. Pack quickly."

"Dad, are we going by helicopter?"

"Yes dear."

"Where are we going?"

"We are going f...ar away."

"Do we have school holidays."

"It is holiday from now on."

"When will we be back?"

"We won't come back."

"Why?"

"Why? Pakistan— don't you know Pakistan? Both Pakistan and China joined together and waged a war against us. In this many people died. We are not yet... dead."

Nitya spoke from inside, "Is it a must to say all this to the child?"

"He must know, Nitya!"

Kumar thought for a moment and said, "Why do we have to leave for another city for that?"

"A lot of poisonous gas has come out of the crackers they burst. It is moving towards us."

"Did we not shoot them?"

"Mmm… we also shot them. It was all fun. We burst bombs like it was Diwali. Karachi, Rawalpindi, Lahore, Peking !"

"Why did we stop?"

"All our crackers got exhausted."

"Dad, get me also one when we reach the new city."

"What?"

"An atom bomb."

Atma laughed, "You are the true leader."

"Kumar, Kumar did you take your things?"

"Yes, mom!" He showed his small school bag. It contained his slate, pencil, eraser, the string for the top, match box, labels, stamps and marbles…."

"Is that all?"

"That's all Dad. Jillu also needs some space. Is it not so?"

Realizing his name was spoken, Jillu, who was lying under the cot, came out suddenly with his ears lifted and wagged his tail at Kumar.

"Jillu, shake hands!"Jillu lifted a leg.

"Jillu, walk … walk."

Jillu stood on two legs and walked four steps.

A small dog, just like a doll with jet black eyes and shaggy hair but with a sweet smell ... a ball of happiness.

Kumar played with it, without any inhibitions. He hugged the dog, pulled its ears, tumbled over it giggling and pulled its legs. But Jillu didn't mind all this. He just stuck to him with pleasure ... two happy children.

"Jillu! Jillu! Dad, are we taking Jillu also with us?"

"No dear, we are leaving him behind."

"What lies! Mummy said that we can take him with us."

"It is your mother who told a lie. There is not enough space in the helicopter for people. They won't let Jillu inside."

Kumar immediately started crying. He hugged the dog and said, "I am not coming."

"You have to come with us. There will be nobody here."

"Both Jillu and I will stay at home. You people can go and come back later."

Nitya came and said, "What is the fight about? Why are you crying, Kumar?"

"Mummy, he says... he says, Jillu cannot be taken."

"Who said so? We are definitely taking Jillu with us. You go inside dear."

Kumar wiped his tears, lifted the dog and went inside with indecision and worry writ large on his face.

"Why do you tell lies to the child? Don't you know that they won't let the dog inside?"

"Why to tell him? I thought of pacifying him at the last moment while taking him away. You just let the cat out of the bag."

"No Nitya. We have to teach him to face disappointments. We cannot supply dreams indefinitely. He should know what the present world is like. He should get the strength of mind."

"Bullshit … as if all these are required at the age of seven. Look here, he is still a baby. He would be very badly upset if he knows that we are leaving the dog behind. He is very emotionally attached to him. He will fall sick. We will somehow or other manage at the last moment. Just keep telling him we are taking the dog with us."

Another two hours passed.

From inside the room they heard Kumar. "Jillu, don't be scared… I'll take you with me. I won't leave you … If they don't let you in, we can shoot them."

Nitya said all of a sudden. "Why can't we do like this?"

"What?"

"There is still some space in the box. Why not wrap him in a towel…"

"No, he will die, just by mere wailing."

"Are we allowed a basket in hand?"

"Look here Nitya, don't complicate things unnecessarily. Let's leave him here. It will pose a problem for food. Had I been a Westerner, he would have been shot by now. I too don't like to leave the pet here all by himself. What to do? The bastards have created havoc in their hurry."

"Atma, please!"

It was five by the time they left. The black cloud had grown slightly larger. Atma, Nitya and Kumar came out and waited. Atma took a last look around at their small independent open house, the trellis of jasmine, mango tree, *makizha* (tree bearing sweet scented flowers) and the small nameplate RS Atma on the door.

"I don't remember whether I switched off the gas or not."

"Shit, hurry up. Whether the gas is closed or not, what does it matter?"

A box and a small basket…

Basket !

"Hey! what is in the basket?"

"Shhhh… be quiet. Jillu is sleeping. We can manage."

"Look here, unnecessary problem! It would be embarrassing if they open the basket. No, leave it." He pulled at the basket. Kumar screamed.

"Leave it, I'll manage. It seems they don't check."

The army's three ton truck came and stopped in front of them. A uniformed voice said, "Come, come quick, quick."

Atma, Nitya and Kumar, with their box and basket got in and the truck started moving. Atma looked at the others—all worried faces! Faces which do not know what the future holds. Where are we going, where will we stand, which direction, which soil? Not knowing anything….

The rattling vehicle reached the helipad and joined the slow moving queue. Officers in army uniform were moving up and down. All the seven helicopters had seven queues. Everybody from the city, without any differences, tottered and climbed on to the unknown entrance with a lot of anxiety and hurry. The young army officers helped the old to get in. People standing, walking, wheel chairs, walking sticks, poor people, children..... the whole city would be evacuated in the next one hour.

As Atma, Nitya and Kumar neared the mechanical bird, he felt his anxiety mounting. If only they could get into the helicopter and take off without any problem, then they could manage half-hearted smiles.

Closer and closer.

The officer said, "Just a box only?"

"A box and this basket." The basket was covered with a towel.

The military personnel lifted the box, examined it and said, "Get in quick."

"Thank god!"

Nitya lifted the basket. Just at that time, Jillu who had been sleeping till then started whimpering.

"Nitya , get in quickly!"

Now Jillu started howling clearly and loudly.

"Just a minute, ma'am."

The junior officer snatched the basket from her and swiftly removed the towel covering the basket.

"Dog!" He picked up Jillu and kept him on the table.

"My god! Whose is this?"

Atma said, "Officer, it is like this. My son...."

"Were you people not told repeatedly? Was it not announced through the loud speaker? Was not a door to door message given?

Only the most essential things are to be taken. Dog! God, what stupidity, I say!"

"Officer, please, listen to me, my son ..."

"Look Mister, I have no time to argue with you. Can you see the clouds? Radiation. Radio-active rain is closing in on us. We are all just a few miles away from death. There is not enough space for human beings and you want to bring your pet dog. If we give into your request, that man would like to bring his piano, another one would argue why he has to leave his milch cow? We are all running away for survival. Our CO is angry with me because I sanctioned 8 kgs to each of you. No dog. Cannot be permitted."

Nitya said, "This is like our child."

"Get inside! Get inside! No dog ! Next, next."

Atma said, "You wretch."

"What?"

"The war was waged only because of you people. You threw an atom bomb on them, in a hurry, without thinking about the repercussions. They threw one in retaliation. It is because of the hasty actions of savage citizens like you... because of your murderous zeal, that wars occur and we innocent people get caught, die, get separated, deported, run from city to city leaving all our precious possessions. Bloody, military rascals, bastards..."

Atma was given a resounding slap on his cheek.

"Look Mister, we are not responsible. It is the leaders who are responsible. Haul him up, I say."

Atma was hauled up like a bundle and stuffed inside. Nitya

was also pulled up followed by others in a hurry. Finally, the officer got in and the door closed.

The rotor blade started rotating, the rotating movement gained momentum and the helicopters, one after another climbed up in a military formation.

Nitya asked, "Atma, does it hurt?" Far too many people were crowded inside. Both Nitya and Atma were stuck in a corner and held on to whatever was available. As the helicopter climbed higher and higher, fear got entangled in the pit of their stomach.

Atma said, "Kumar, we can buy a new dog when we go to the new city."

"Kumar?"

"Hey Kumar … Nitya where is Kumar?"

"He was with you."

"No ...he was holding your hand."

"Kumar… Kumar! Kumaaa...r."

Nitya's screaming melted with the machine's noise.

"Sir, please sir, my son! We have left our son behind. Open the door… open please…"

So saying, Atma banged against the door. A strong hand slapped him, pushed him and caught hold of him.

Helicopters disappeared like a dot in the sky. Kumar, who was hiding under the bench, came out carrying Jillu.

"Don't worry, Jillu. Daddy and Mummy will return after a few days. Let's go home."

Both the little boy and the dog, slowly but cheerfully walked towards their house. On the way, Kumar picked up a few cookies from the unmanned cookie shop, gave one to Jillu and ate the others. As they were walking towards their house, they both got happily drenched in the rain which started pouring at that time.